HER NAME WAS
DOLORES

HER NAME WAS DOLORES

THE *Jenn* I KNEW

PETE SALGADO *y* GABRIEL VÁZQUEZ

HarperCollins *Español*

Editor-in-Chief: *Graciela Lelli*
Interior design: *Grupo Nivel Uno, Inc.*

ISBN: 978-0-71809-643-4

Printed in the United States of America

17 18 19 20 21 DCI 7 6 5 4 3 2 1

Contents

Introduction 7

1. The End and the Beginning 13
2. Becoming Perfectly Imperfect.........................25
3. Life on the Road 43
4. Love and Music 63
5. La Gran Señora Conquers Mexico...................83
6. Trials and Tribulations.......................................99
7. Bossing It Up! A Business Magnate
    in the Making... 111
8. Success Comes at a Price............................. 131
9. Unforgettable Baby 157
10. Happily Ever After? Love, Loss, and Betrayals.......... 173
11. Paloma Negra.. 207
12. Lights Out 223
13. The Aftermath 237

Epilogue: Jenni Rivera's Legacy................................ 257
Acknowledgments.. 265
About the Authors 269

Introduction

jennirivera
@jennirivera

A Diva Delivers..always! Damage,
Deception, Divorce.. Ding Dongs and
Dip shits... Don't Stop Her. A Diva
DOES...Always. Diamond in Da ruff?
Nahh...she's a Full blown DIAMOND
whom Decides the value of her karats
her Damn Self. Yup.... A Diva
DELIVERS. #DivaFACTS

2012-10-17

I n September 2012, just a few months before Jenni Rivera's fatal plane crash, Jen's career was as hot as it gets. She was at the top of her game musically, she had TV deals and fans that numbered in the millions, and she was selling out arenas on the regular, but her personal life was in complete disarray. Her complicated matrix of relationships, which had always been fraught with different levels of disappointment and betrayal, was now spinning out of control before her eyes, and everything reached a boiling point around the time Jen was killed in that jet. Maybe it was because of her extreme celebrity, or because of the catastrophic quality of the accident. Perhaps it was because of the fanfare and sadness and everything that comes with such an unexpected tragedy. Whatever the reason, after her death, no one spoke up about what was really unfolding in Jen's life at the time of her death. Until now. I'm here to lay it on the line and give it to you straight.

After Jenni Rivera passed away on December 9, 2012, my nights were peppered with vivid dreams that haunted my waking hours. I tried to decipher these apparitions of my beloved old friend and sister by choice, but wasn't sure how to interpret them. All I know is that they moved me to the deepest core of my heart and soul and will forever be etched in my memory. The first one took place on a mountaintop. Jen and I stood together overlooking the entire city below. She was wearing a beautiful white gown and kept repeating, "It's okay. It had to be this way, and it's okay. Don't worry." I glanced in her direction, speechless, frozen in place. As she continued repeating this statement, tears streamed down my face, we turned back to the view of the city lights before us, and I woke up.

In another dream, she showed up in her casual sweat suit, the warmups she lived in when the spotlight was off, and once again said to me, "It's okay, it had to be this way, don't worry." Then she added a classic Jenni phrase, "Tell the kids to knock their shit off," and ended it with, "Tell Rosie to be sure to listen." If I was a betting man, I would bet my last dollar that the person in this dream was really Jen. As her words melted into my consciousness, I suddenly felt my wife by my side waking me and asking, "Are you okay?" She had felt me murmuring in my sleep, struggling to speak in my dream to no avail. Jen's presence was as strong as ever. I felt she had just visited me, but as wonderful as it was to see her again, it also stirred up endless amounts of pain from the reality of her recent death. Nevertheless, rather than sweeping these dreams under the rug or deleting them from my memories, I decided to hold on to them and replay them in my mind.

I was unable to speak in these dreams, so maybe Jen's point was for me to listen. Were these just dreams, or could they really be a message I should take to heart? While I pondered the possibilities, the dreams stopped as abruptly as they'd begun … until four years later, when I began working on this book and the Univision series about Jen's life. It was a sign. As worried as I had been about broaching these projects to the best of my ability and knowledge, I believe Jen would've wanted me to speak the truth in her straight-shooting, no holds barred fashion. The time has come for the Jen I knew to see the light of day.

Besides being her close friend and manager, I wore many hats in Jen's life. I was her security. I was her advisor. I was her ride. I was her balance. I was her backup. I was her right hand. I was her sounding board. I was her brother. And given these many roles, I was intimately caught in the web of her personal issues, including problems with her kids, siblings, parents, husbands, and friends. I was there for support, damage control, or just to lend an ear and make her feel safe.

There was a lot of shit going down behind closed doors. It was far from a perfect life, but Jen never felt the need to hide any of this because she knew it made her who she was. After her passing, it seemed everyone and their mother came out of the woodworks trying to become Jen's voice, trying to tell their picture-perfect version of her story, trying to apologize for her mistakes. But I know Jen, and she wasn't one to apologize. She stood her ground and didn't back down, unless she believed making amends was the right choice, because no matter how stubborn she was, she also had a huge heart and was an incredibly loyal friend. The world saw her as a force to be reckoned with, but she was actually a soft and gentle soul, and one of her deepest secrets was simply her vulnerability.

Now, let me make one thing clear before we go on. This book is not intended to shame Jen's family or anyone else for that matter. I just want to clarify and explain the complexity behind Jen's life. I want you to join me in celebrating her strengths and acknowledging her weaknesses so that you can fully understand the perfectly imperfect beauty behind her magic. Jenni the Diva was not an overnight success. Her outstanding career was a product of love, tireless work, and endless battles. She demolished all the road blocks, pummeled all the naysayers, and beat all the odds to shatter several glass ceilings and rise to the top. That's why this book is so important to me. In reading Jen's official autobiography, one that her family finished writing for her after her death, I felt it was chock-full of lipstick. But that wasn't Jen. The Jen that I knew wasn't about a lot of lipstick; she was raw and real. That's what her fans loved about her, and that's what I'm hoping to convey in these pages.

It took me four years to share my Jen story because at first I felt an inherent need to protect her, but now I realize that her life and legacy are meant to be shared and celebrated. I have no ulterior motives. As her close friend and brother by choice, I simply want to do right by her, and if I have to take any heat, I'm ready, as ready as Jen would've been if she were here with us today. All I want is for you, the reader, the fan, the admirer, the curious onlooker, to feel and understand the ups and downs, the ins and outs, and the tears and laughs that made Jen the stellar artist and human being we all grew to know and love. It was a tough ride, but worth absolutely every second of it. May these pages bring you some sense of closure and may they inspire you not only to keep Jenni Rivera's legacy alive and thriving, but also to accomplish your lifelong goals and dreams, no matter how difficult the journey ahead. I know that's what the Jenni I knew would've wanted for you, so, taking a page from her story, don't let anyone or anything ever hold you back … and make sure to enjoy the ride.

Chapter 1

The End and the Beginning

 **Jenni Rivera** ✓
@jennirivera

RT @petesalgado: @jennirivera WE
BOUT TO CHANGE D GAME
AGAIN! /// God has plans!

8/16/12, 4:12 PM

J enni crouched down, sat on a parking lot wheel stop
outside the hospital, and slowly looked up at me, her dark
brown eyes brimming with pain and heartache, simply
broken.

"Are you okay?" I asked her.

"Yeah, I'm fine," she said as she glanced away.

"No, you can't lie to me. Your eyes always tell me the truth."

Jenni's eyes were the mirrors to her soul; one glance and I
could see through all the smiles and jokes and bullshit and know
how she was really feeling.

"Ah, badass Pete, I hate when you do that to me," she replied
in classic Jenni style.

When asked about the last time I saw Jenni Rivera, I inevitably go back to that day, November 28, 2012. My father had just passed away a few hours earlier, and Jenni—my steadfast, kind, giving, loyal, longtime friend—was there, right by my side, offering my family and me her moral support. My father's death was not sudden, it was not unexpected, he had been sick for a while, and we knew it was imminent. So we were incredibly fortunate to be by his side, surrounding him with love, encouraging him to let go, reassuring him that we would be okay, and I had the honor and privilege of holding his hand as he took his last breath and left this world. This type of loss is far from easy, but there was a sense of peace and closure that enveloped my family and me that day, one that we were also able to transmit to my father as he passed on, one that I only wish Jenni could've had when her life came to a crashing end.

That evening, after lending her love and support and taking a few hours out of her busy schedule to be by our side, when it was time for Jenni to head home, my wife and I walked her out to her car in the hospital parking lot, making small talk along the way. When she sat on that wheel stop and our eyes met, I knew something was up, but she was hesitant to open up to us, even though this was something she did on a regular basis at home. However, now, she felt that since my father had just passed, it wasn't appropriate for her to bring up her problems, but I insisted. I could see my friend was in far deeper pain than I and in need of someone to lean on, maybe even a shoulder to cry on. This was one of the core foundations of our friendship: we constantly supported each other through the good and the bad; we always had each other's backs. I was in a peaceful state of mind that evening, so I encouraged her to tell me what was weighing her down and causing her eyes to communicate such profound sadness. It was a little tug of war because she didn't want to break down in my time of need, but she finally let it pour out.

In the close to ten years that I have known Jen, as I used to call her, I have seen her experience a roller coaster of intense, painful, and sad moments in her life. The trial of her first ex-husband, José Trinidad Marín, for sexually abusing her sister and daughters; the incarceration and death of Juan Lopez, her second ex-husband and the father of her two youngest children; her soul mate's battle with drug addiction; the rape charges against her son, Mikey; the demise of her third marriage ... these were all heart-wrenching events, but I had never seen her so utterly hurt and distraught, so emotionally gutted as on that day at the hospital.

Our Hood Queen, la Diva, la Gran Señora, the fighter, the survivor, the woman who everyone, from fans to friends to family, deemed as unbreakable was falling apart before my eyes. As she shared what was in her heart that night, she confessed that she still carried a sense of endless guilt about the abuse her sister and daughters had suffered at the hands of her ex-husband, Trino. She wished she had figured it out sooner, she wished she could've done something to stop it, but when she finally found out, more than ten years later, it was too late, for the damage had been done. As we delved further into these events that forever changed the life of her sister and daughters, as well as her own existence, I urged her to let go of all that guilt once and for all. It did her no good and drove her to overcompensate with her children in ways that proved to be unhealthy for all of them.

"You have to forgive yourself. You have to forgive yourself, Jen. You have to." I kept repeating this phrase, hoping to get the message across to her. I just wanted to see her happy again.

"You know, Pete, I've finally accepted that I was also a victim. I was fifteen years old. The first time I even had sex, I ended up pregnant, and he was in his twenties. What did I know?"

She was right, and she'd also suffered domestic abuse, way too much for a teenager to handle, but she somehow managed to keep going. I was glad to see her accepting that she too had been a victim. Then the conversation took a turn into her present life circumstances, the one reason she felt her world had been shattered into a million pieces: her daughter, Chiquis. She was so hurt and in disbelief, trying to come to terms with what she believed was her daughter's ultimate betrayal. At the time, she couldn't have cared less about her soon-to-be ex-husband Esteban. Losing a man had nothing against the possibility of losing a daughter. Chiquis was her blood, her baby, her best friend, her confidant; they had been in the trenches together ever since Jenni gave birth to her at fifteen, so the thought that Chiquis had betrayed her in such a way caused her unbearable pain, disappointment, and shame.

Jen couldn't come to terms with this, she didn't know what to do, she was as lost as I had ever seen her. She didn't want to bring any of this to the public light because, at the end of the day, no matter what happened, Chiquis was her daughter and, even though they were not speaking and Jenni was hurt beyond repair, she would never throw her own flesh and blood under the bus. She would never humiliate her princess in that way; she would always protect her no matter what went down between them. But it was eating her up inside, and she finally let it all out and broke down.

Jenni was the glue in the Rivera family—that is even clearer now than it was back then—she helped keep them all united, yet this time she had no idea how she was going to come back from this latest blow. She was like a broken mirror, you could piece her back together, but the cracks would still be visible. She was devastated.

Sitting before me was a woman who was adored by millions, who had rolled up her sleeves and worked tirelessly for years on end to make her dreams come true, someone who had hit innumerable milestones in her career, who had fought tooth and nail to give her children the life they deserved, who inspired countless women who had been knocked down to get up, dust themselves off, and keep moving forward. Yet that day, those tear-filled eyes told me the real story. Our hard-working, unstoppable Diva de la Banda was feeling completely defeated and lost.

When our conversation finally came to an end, I gave her a big bear hug, and told her I was there for her, always. She was my sister, and I was ready to do anything I could to lift her spirits and help her get her personal life back on track. In retrospect, I'm so grateful we were able to share that meaningful moment, those words, that heart-to-heart conversation. I'm glad I was able to be there for her to help lighten the load she had been carrying those past few months, even if only for a moment. I had faith she would be okay and everything would work itself out. I was sure she would eventually be able to pick herself back up again and move on, as she had done in countless other situations. She just needed a little time to figure it all out, but what I didn't know was that time was no longer on her side.

That day wasn't technically the last day I saw Jen, but it was the last meaningful conversation we had before she left this world, the one I will never forget. The actual last time I saw her was on December 5, 2012, during the taping of her radio show, *Contacto directo con Jenni Rivera*, which she taped every Wednesday. She was scheduled to fly to Mexico the following day—Thursday, December 6, 2012—so I stopped by the station to iron out last-minute details before she left. Her dad was a guest on the show that day; she had actually asked him to come with her, but he had to stay behind to take care of some business.

It was another typical day in Jenni's life, but she was super excited about this particular show in Monterrey because it was yet another milestone in her career. No one in banda music had ever sold out the Monterrey Arena. Selling out that venue was already a huge accomplishment, but doing so in her music genre was a groundbreaking event for her and for banda music in general. She was ecstatic! We went over details after the radio program. I was scheduled to go to Monterrey to oversee production of *I Love Jenni.* It was the first time the show's production team would be traveling with her to Mexico. Needless to say, with my father's passing, I wasn't able to attend. She asked how all of the arrangements were coming along, wanting to make sure that everything was taken care of, checking to see if I was going to be okay, always remembering to stop and care for others no matter what sunny days or stormy weather she was facing in her life. She also mentioned Chiquis in that conversation, but seemed calmer about it all; she was in better spirits.

I actually remember her being so happy that Wednesday, filled with many hopes, dreams, and goals for the following year, ones that would bring her closer to home and her beloved children. I never imagined that would be the last day I would see Jen. I couldn't have even fathomed the shock and loss that we would suffer only a few days later. I gave her a hug and said good-bye, happy to see her up and in better spirits, but I knew she was still grappling with a lot within. I couldn't help but think about that touching, honest, and heartbreaking conversation we'd had a few days earlier. In truth, that no-holds-barred woman who sat on that wheel stop in that hospital parking lot, pouring her heart out and expressing her deepest regrets and emotions, that there wasn't Jenni Rivera the Diva, la Gran Señora, or La Reina de Long Beach. Her name was Dolores, and that there was the Jen that I knew and loved.

It was ten a.m. on another sunny California morning in April 2003. I was sitting in a Beverly Hills conference room, where I was scheduled to meet with a singer at my friend Anthony Lopez's request. Anthony was an alumnus from my college, a mentor, and an entertainment attorney who had recently mentioned that he had a possible job opportunity for me. He explained it was the sister of one of his clients who was looking to do something bigger with her music career. She was in the process of assembling her own team, so he asked if I'd be interested in taking a meeting with her. Coming from such a close friend, I said yes without hearing any more details. Then he summed it up for me further: it was Lupillo Rivera's sister, Jenni; she was looking to make a name for herself. I sighed and immediately thought, *Oh, great, another little sister project.* Those are usually tough ones to manage because their careers rarely make it as far as their famous sibling's, but I was already on board for the meeting, so I figured I'd do my friend a solid and see it through. And that's where I was that morning, at Anthony's law office, in a conference room, on time, noticing how the minutes continued to tick by with no Jenni in sight.

Shuffling in my chair, I kept checking my watch. Thirty minutes had gone by and nothing. By the time the clock struck 10:40 a.m., I was annoyed and bordering on angry. Forty minutes late? Talk about a bad first impression. I decided to call it a morning and leave; I had waited long enough. While I gathered my things and prepared to head out, the conference room door suddenly swung open and in stormed a woman like a hurricane, exuding a charm that I had rarely seen before. Thirty-three years old, forty minutes late, fake eyelashes and glue in one hand and a vanity mirror in the other, she apologized for keeping me waiting, sat at the head of the fancy conference table and, while balancing the spiky points of each lash on her sharp acrylic nails, a tiny tangle of swords that she maneuvered with precision, she cut to the chase and got down to business.

She was such a force to be reckoned with that any anger at her for being late dissipated instantly. All I could think was, *What the hell just walked into this room?!* She didn't even give me time to react. I had been ready to take off, but there was something about her, her strength and sweetness, the way she commanded the room with her presence yet didn't gave a damn about what I or anyone else thought about her. Jenni had no qualms, no reservations; if she needed to get something done, she'd do it, regardless of the place or the circumstances, and that included wrapping up her makeup routine while holding a meeting with her possible future manager. I couldn't leave now; my curiosity was piqued. Cool as a cucumber, but wild in the eyes ... *Who is this woman?*

Now, remember, back in those days, we weren't used to Googling people and doing extensive online research before meeting prospective clients, so it was all about that first impression. That was the person's one chance to pitch themselves and give it their all to land the deal. I had mixed emotions from the get-go. On one hand, I was completely taken aback, surprised, and intrigued by the situation, definitely not what I was expecting; on the other, I was chuckling at the whole scene in disbelief: *Who does this?* However, as she began to introduce herself, I quickly noticed she expressed herself clearly and eloquently, and man did she have charisma. That was the clincher right there. If I've learned anything in my many years in the music business is that no matter how hard you try, you can't buy or learn how to be charismatic. You either have it or you don't; it's that simple. And Jenni had it by the truckloads. The minute she walked into the room, her charisma took over. Forty minutes late and instead of being upset, I was completely captivated by her persona, paying attention to her every word. Her confidence and charm instantly won me over. I was so impressed that instead of leaving, I perked up in my chair and honed in on what she had to say.

After apologizing for being late, blaming it on the traffic and the long drive from Corona, where she lived at the time, she immediately opened up about her marital issues. I came to find out she was the mother of five and in the middle of her second divorce from a guy who had also been her manager. Jenni was honest and forthright, she explained how her soon-to-be-ex was blatantly trying to rob her, but she didn't do so to garner pity. She wasn't playing the victim. She was just laying it all on the table for me to get a better sense of who she was and where she was coming from. Right away Jenni felt like this force, a woman who showed more balls than many other men I've dealt with. She came across as determined to win, like some kind of brown Super Woman who would be nobody's fool and was hell-bent on pushing forward as an artist and performer.

Jenni continued her pitch and gave it to me straight. She was ready to take her career to the next level. She wanted to get out of the nightclubs and start playing major venues, she planned to release a cosmetics line, she hoped to do apparel, she spoke about getting into TV and radio, she dreamed about selling out the Gibson Amphitheater ... she wanted to stop being known as Lupillo Rivera's sister and finally come into her own as Jenni Rivera. She had a clear vision, she had ambition, she was ready to roll up her sleeves and do the work, and she knew that in order to accomplish her dreams and goals, she needed to assemble her own team, one that was solely dedicated to her career.

There was an immediate fierceness about Jenni, a casual round-the-way-girl kind of swagger that at once commanded respect, but also made you feel like you were her blood. I vibed well with her from the start; we were both straight-shooters and ambitious dreamers determined to make our wishes a reality. I understood that she was in the throes of a life transition—personally, professionally, and creatively—and she needed someone to step in and be her sounding board and right-hand man. She knew she was on the brink of something big and needed help to get there.

Meanwhile, I was coming off a successful run with Los Tucanes de Tijuana, a popular Mexican Regional group. As a successful business manager, I had catapulted them into major sponsorships with Coors and had landed them a deal at a major record label.

They were booming, at the height of their success, and I felt that I had hit the roof with them, so it was time to move on.

Early on, I dove into the Latin market when I noticed it was in dire need of professional business managers. Back in the day, most managers were usually *compadres*, friends of the artists who were winging it and going along for the ride, but they didn't understand the U.S. market because they hadn't been educated here. So that was my opening. I found my niche. I had a business degree under my belt, knew the local and national business laws, and I understood the gringos. It was a match made in heaven. Prior to Los Tucanes de Tijuana, I had the chance to work with the likes of Juan Gabriel and Joan Sebastián. By the time I met Jenni, my résumé was on point and impressive, and she knew it. Jenni had heard about my success with other great artists, and she was hopeful that I would be able to do something with her too. She was ready and so was I.

From the moment I met her, I felt her bigger-than-life presence, and I knew in my gut that we would create something phenomenal together. And we did. We made everything she mentioned in that meeting a reality throughout her career. From the beginning, she told me the end. I was in the presence of the future Diva, la Gran Señora, the star, but that day I also met Jenni the woman, the hustler, the person who was going to provide for her family no matter what it took, filled with ambition and dreams for a better life for her loved ones.

She had a vision, and I experienced firsthand the blood, sweat, and tears that she shed along the way to make it become a reality. Never would I have imagined, on that first day, how far we would come. Number one hits, international tours, countless career milestones, love, heartbreak, danger, betrayal, and ultimately death. A telenovela has nothing on Jenni's life because her story was real, not fiction. And even when she took one too many punches and was down for the count, she managed to rise to the occasion, making barrels of lemonade out of all the sour lemons thrown her way. She was everyone's team captain, she kept the boat afloat and on course; she was our leader, our inspiration, and our friend.

Yet, in all honesty, at first I had my doubts. I wasn't sure if a woman who arrived forty minutes late to such an important meeting was up to the task. Was she really ready to take this seriously enough to push her career to the next level? I was somewhat skeptical, but also intrigued. She commanded that room like a pro, had clear goals, and had major cojones. This was no damsel in distress, she didn't need saving, she knew exactly where she wanted to go and how she planned to get there, and she was ready to work elbow-to-elbow to get the job done. But she was smart enough to also realize she couldn't do it all alone. She needed a team, and that's where I came in; Jenni knew that I could help her. She was a diamond in the rough, a butterfly in the making, and she knew she had what it takes to make it. After her pitch, I believed her, I was sold.

"Are you down with me? Are you on board?" she asked after wrapping up her intro and pitch.

"Yeah," I replied, without hesitation, "let's do it."

"Good, let's get to work."

Chapter 2

Becoming Perfectly Imperfect

Jenni Rivera ✔
@jennirivera

"Yo soy siempre YO...sin miedo"...

🌐 Translate from Spanish

9/1/12, 6:48 PM

270 RETWEETS **178** LIKES

↩   ⇄   ♥   •••

T he next meeting I had with Jen was at the recording
studio. She had asked me to swing by to listen to her
latest album, *Homenaje a las grandes*, which was being
mastered and prepped for release. We sat down and ran through
the songs. It was the first time I heard Jenni sing. I honestly wasn't
impressed by her voice. Her lower register hadn't developed
yet, so it was a bit thin and tinny, but I knew that was something
she could refine and smooth out with time, so I paid attention to
the tunes themselves, the song choices, the message she was
sending with this album.

As her new manager, I had to get to know Jenni before moving forward. I had to analyze her as an artist, assessing the pros and cons in her career and what she had to offer. I already knew, from the get-go, that one of Jenni's unique qualities was her dualities and how naturally she navigated these opposing waters. She was a mom, but at the same time, more like a dad. She was a guy's girl, at once feminine and tough, and both aggressive and forgiving. Jen could be elegant, but she could be hood to the bone. She was rooted in her Mexican-ness, but unequivocally American. The Mexican-American artists on the scene usually focused on the U.S. side of the border, but I knew that Jenni had the potential to cater to audiences on both sides. Jenni was fluent not only in both languages, but in both cultures. She got what it meant to be American, and she also knew what it was to be Mexican, so our main challenge was figuring out how she could speak to both audiences. I quickly realized that for her to make this happen, she first had to find her voice. It was somewhat of a no-brainer: that was the missing piece of this puzzle, that's all we needed to complete her crossover and transform her into an instant outright success.

With *Homenaje a las grandes*, I could tell Jenni was already beginning to let her personality shine through in her music career, not in the songs themselves, but in the album cover. She had ditched the cowboy hat and embraced her Chicana vibe, going for a less traditional image, one that better reflected who she was, with a simple white shirt and silver hoop earrings. Now she needed to do the same with her song choices.

I listened to the songs carefully, but there was no real Jenni Rivera in any of them. It was basically a cover album, somewhat like a highly produced karaoke record. There was no clear sense

of direction, and she wasn't putting herself out there and giving
the audience a piece of the real Jenni, but the album was only
weeks from being released, so there was nothing to be done now.
As I listened, I said, "Wow, that's great, it's great," because I didn't
want to dishearten her, but now I knew what we had to tackle
first. It's not that she couldn't sing covers of other people's songs,
but she needed to bring it to another level, she needed to put
her stamp on them, she needed to own them to the point where
people thought those songs were actually hers, and she needed
to let that open, transparent, no-holds-barred personality of hers
shine through her music. The time had come for her to discover
and communicate who she really was; that was what would
ultimately create that special bond with her fans, which would be
forged through life and even survive her death.

After hearing the last song, I couldn't hold back any longer
and just gave it to her straight. That was the beauty of our
relationship from the start: there were no secrets, and because of
this, that sense of bonding between us only grew stronger with
time. So, I was up front and just put it out there, "Hey, Jen, so the
music sounds great, but I think you need to start defining who you
are. You need to decide what path you want to take and what you
want to say to your audience because there's no real message
here. You're just taking a bunch of songs you like and putting
them together in an album." She listened attentively. I told her
I wanted her to do her homework for the next album. I wanted
her to search for the meaning behind the songs, to see what
resonated with her, what rung true to her soul. I needed her to
connect with the songs on a much more guttural level in order to
make them her own. I also asked her to think about what message
she wanted to give her fans; that was also a crucial decision, one

that she could then clearly portray through her music, both with her future song selections and eventually her own songs. The time had come for Jenni to open up, get in touch with her roots, and sing her story straight from her heart.

For me to help her in this journey to discover her own uniqueness and define the artist she could be, I had to get to know more of her backstory, and that's how Jenni Rivera the hustler, the mother, the provider was slowly revealed before my eyes.

Jenni Rivera was born in Los Angeles on July 2, 1969, to her Mexican parents Pedro and Rosa Rivera. Her brother Gustavo had been born a year earlier, and she was later followed by Lupillo, Pedro, Juan, and Rosie. I was privy to the inner workings of the Rivera family for more than a decade and can say they are quite a unique bunch. Don Pedro and Rosa were both musicians, obligated to cast aside those dreams to fulfill their traditional obligations. Rosa followed protocol: she got married, had kids, and instead of becoming a *cantante*, she took on the role of mother and housewife. Don Pedro set aside his personal dreams as a singer and entertainer to comply with the obligations as husband, father, and family provider. They crossed the border and established themselves in California to pursue their American Dream, both of them rolling up their sleeves to work as hard as needed to give their children a better life, while also making sure they were actively involved in music from a young age, likely hoping to someday live out their musical dreams vicariously through them.

As with many large families, the children were constantly competing for their parents' attention, but they had a competitiveness among them like I'd never seen before, both a blessing and a burden in their lives. It's all good when you're in the spotlight, but it sure isn't easy when your life unfolds in the shadows of that light. Jen had the chance to be on both sides of this coin, so she knew all this too well, and hopped to it from a young age.

Jenni knew that the way to her dad's heart was through music. That was her "in," that was the way she would capture his attention and stand out among her siblings. So as a young girl, when she started singing, Don Pedro perked up his ears and immediately felt this was his chance to turn her into a star. He drove her to different talent contests to perform onstage, hoping that someone might discover his little *reina*. But at one of these shows, when Jenni was eleven, the unthinkable happened: she walked on stage, ready to compete, yet when the music started playing, her mind drew a complete blank. Nothing, nada, zilch, silence. She not only forgot the lyrics, she forgot the lyrics to a song she knew like the back of her hand, she forgot the lyrics to a song that years later would become one of her number one radio hits, "Besos y copas."

Jenni ran off stage, in disbelief of what had just happened to her. She was devastated, to say the least, and the drive home proved to be pure torture. Don Pedro scolded her nonstop—how could she have forgotten the lyrics to a song she knew so well! … he'd taught her better than that … what she had done up there was totally unprofessional and inexcusable, she should've known better—going on and on about what in Jenni's short eleven years of life had been the most humiliating moment ever. She stared out the window as she heard her father's raging flood of harsh words, and tears welled up in those big brown eyes as she took the verbal beating. It wasn't the humiliation of the experience that upset her, but rather her father's disappointment in her. All she wanted was to make him happy and proud. The whole point of participating in these singing competitions was to spend time with him and enjoy his undivided attention. Music was supposed to bring them together, so when she felt she had failed him and noticed it was having the opposite effect on their relationship, she simply up and quit. Jenni turned to her dad right then and there and vowed to never sing on any stage ever again. The tears rolled down her cheeks freely now. She'd had enough. Little did she know that, twelve years later, the tide would turn, and she would be grabbing the mic once again, embarking on what would be the start of her passion and career for the rest of her life.

But back then her mind had been made up. She shelved her musical inclinations and moved on with her budding adolescence. However, only four years later, in 1984, after Jen turned fifteen, the unthinkable happened: she got pregnant. By 1985 she had moved out of her house, was living with her husband José Trinidad Marín, aka Trino, and was giving birth to her first daughter, Chiquis. She was only sixteen. Meanwhile, her relationship quickly took an abusive turn. Aside from putting her down verbally, Trino started beating her, yet Jen wasn't about to take that lying down. She was a fighter, and she knew how to throw a punch. She had grown up with four brothers and learned at a young age how to defend herself. So when Trino went at her, she hit him right back. It was not pretty, but Jen was young and she didn't know any better.

What she thought was the final straw came in 1989 when Trino started beating her while she was five months pregnant with her second child, Jacqie. That night she grabbed Chiquis and left him. She asked her brother Gus if she could rent out his garage, and that's where they settled in for the next few months. Those were harrowing times for Jen, one of those low points she never forgot no matter how successful she became later. Not only was she pregnant and living in a garage with her four-year-old daughter, but her car was stolen right before her eyes, and her insurance didn't cover theft, so now she was wheel-less in a city whose distances require a car. She had no choice but to bite the bullet and buy a bicycle—there was no way she could afford another car under those circumstances. So her ten-speed bike was her new means of transportation. She'd wake up bright and early every morning, bike Chiquis to daycare, then ride to work. Jen was a survivor, so she learned to make due with whatever she had at hand. Finally, Don Pedro found out about her situation and asked her to move back home before she had her second daughter and, although Jen was incredibly proud, she accepted. She knew it would be in Chiquis's best interest to live in a normal home and close to her beloved aunt Rosie.

Then, the tides seemed to take a turn for the better. Jen had received her associate's degree, had become a licensed real estate agent, and had landed a job at Century 21. She was finally able to breathe again and actually managed to purchase her first home, but in the process she also got back together with Trino. They had another baby together in 1991, this time a boy, Mikey, and she thought they were finally on track to becoming a normal family. But instead of getting better, things got worse. The fights began to escalate again, and by 1992 she finally left Trino for good, not knowing the gut-wrenching damage he had caused her family, something she would discover years later.

In the scope of things, 1992 was a big year for Jen. She not only managed to end the abusive relationship with her husband, she also unknowingly took the first steps toward what would become her future bread and butter: on a dare, while out with friends, after twelve years of vowing to never sing again, she climbed on stage at the nightclub El Rancho Grande, asked the norteño band to play Chalino Sánchez's "Nieves de enero," and belted it out to a cheering crowd. As she walked down those steps and felt that performance high, she was flooded with memories of how much she loved singing and realized how much she had missed it. But she still didn't consider she could make a career out of it.

She was so happy to have reconnected with music that, shortly after that quick stint on stage, she recruited her brothers to help her record an album for her dad as a birthday gift, her first one, *Somos Rivera*. Don Pedro had founded a successful record label a few years earlier, and everyone in the family had chipped in at some point or other by working at the office, including Jenni. Suffice to say, they had access to recording studios and knew what they were doing. Don Pedro was so happy he started promoting *Somos Rivera* around town, hoping to make a name for Jenni in the industry. Meanwhile, the real estate business had taken a nosedive, and Jenni was once again hitting another low point in her life. She had to bite the bullet and go on welfare in order to make ends meet for herself and her three children.

Since she had dipped her toes back into the music world, Jenni agreed to play a gig as the opening act to an artist who was on her father's label, but was horrified when she tried to get paid and the manager propositioned her. He basically said she had to have sex with him before he could pay her. She'd had enough. She was about ready to hang her mic up again, when Don Pedro begged her to record one more album for him. She couldn't say no to her beloved dad, so she recorded *Por un amor*, which captured the attention of Balboa Records. So she signed on with them to record another album, *La Maestra*, but they did nothing to promote it.

By 1994, Jen had another stroke of luck: the real estate market picked up, and she was out of the hole and once again making a decent living for her family. She was still interested in music, but putting food on the table and providing for her three children was (and has always been) her main priority, and music wasn't about to feed them just yet.

A year later, in 1995, she met her soon-to-be second husband, Juan Lopez and started another tumultuous relationship that lasted eight years. He wasn't physically abusive like Trino, but they did butt heads and fight passionately. He became her manager in her slow-budding music career, and she had two more children with him, Jenicka in 1997, and Johnny in 2001. The same year Jen met Juan, she had a hit, "La Chacalosa," in the underground music scene, which garnered her L.A. fans. At this point, Jenni was active in the business world. She wasn't about to give up her Century 21 job, but she wasn't going to say no to easy money either. Sing some songs and get a five-hundred-dollar paycheck? Hey, why not? It meant more money in the bank while doing something she loved, so she kept at it.

When the end of the nineties rolled in, Don Pedro took her material to Que Buena, the local radio station in L.A. dedicated to Spanish-language Regional Mexican music, but they were hesitant to play her music. Jen's brother, Lupillo Rivera, was making a name for himself in the music industry, and they didn't want to oversaturate the airwaves with too many Riveras. However, Jenni did get some airplay at other stations. Her following continued to slowly grow, and she started getting more offers to play at local clubs. Being the hustler that she was, she kept saying yes to the gigs. They meant more money for her children, and it didn't hurt that she was also doing what she loved.

Finally, around 2001, Que Buena decided to play Jen's music. She was over the moon. The airplay then extended to other counties and states. That's when Jen's keen entrepreneurial sense kicked in; she saw this as a business opportunity and ran with it. Juan and Jen quit their daytime jobs and dedicated themselves full-time to her music career. It was now or never, do or die. Unfortunately, this was also the beginning of the end of their relationship. After many fights, infidelities, and other issues, which I will get into later in this book, Jenni decided to file for divorce in 2003. This also coincided with her wanting to break away from the family music business, put together her own team, and carve her own path. She knew she could go further and do more, she knew she had what it took—she just needed the right team to get her there.

So there we were, 2003, in the studio, putting together a plan to turn Jenni the underground sensation into Jenni Rivera the international star. However, we still had a few roadblocks to conquer. After garnering some success with "Las Malandrinas," one of her first groundbreaking *corridos*, and having done some tours, she was ready for more. But at the time there was still a fair amount of bias and prejudice against women—especially in Mexico, a country she hoped to win over with her music one day.

They wouldn't even consider putting her on TV there. She wasn't a teen act in short-shorts with her boobs out, so that pretty much made her irrelevant in the Mexican media. I knew she was never going to be that type of act—she knew it, too. It just wasn't who she was and that was the main challenge: getting people to see her for the woman she was rather than just *la hermana de Lupillo* (Lupillo's sister).

Her brother Lupillo had skyrocketed to fame. He had gone platinum and was the first person to really make it in the music industry within their family. This made everyone immediately turn their attention to him. He was the golden child; all loyalty and hopes and dreams were now focused on Lupillo. Don Pedro's record label, Cintas Acuarios, was still up and running and doing well, but the wealth of family resources that one would think Jenni had at her disposal to forward her career were actually hard to come by for Jen. She got little to no attention from this team because it really was all about Lupillo. On the other hand, she had a popular brother in an industry that she was trying to break into, but had little to no support from him either. Lupillo now had the ability and resources to help Jenni fast-track her career, but rather than lend her a hand, his team would hire other women to open his huge shows, and Jenni had to bite her tongue and continue her journey the old-fashioned way, knocking on doors, dealing with the constant rejection, and also doing all she could to separate her image from that of her famous brother.

It sure as hell wasn't easy. The media had gotten used to referring to her as *la hermana de Lupillo*, and they'd reach out to her not to interview her about her music, but to ask her about the latest news regarding her brother, totally sidelining her talent and musical career. That's all she heard, left and right, that's how promoters presented her on stage, that's how hosts introduced her on the radio, that's how people recognized her in person. Ten years after launching her career, she was still stopped at airports by fans who'd say, "¡Ay, tú eres la hermana de Lupillo!" ("Hey, you're Lupillo's sister!") as they asked for a picture. And I remember her reply like it was yesterday: "I have a name too." So many years, so many sacrifices, so much hard work, and they still saw her as Lupillo's sister? Enough was enough, she was sick of living in his shadow, it was time for a change.

Now, to be clear, she loved her brother dearly and was ecstatic with his success, celebrating each accomplishment with pure joy, but she was also somewhat disappointed and hurt by how things had unfolded between them. She hadn't expected such sibling rivalry, it was a real hard pill to swallow, but that wasn't about to stop Jenni; she picked herself up and moved on. She was never one to wallow in her sadness; she was all about action and taking control of her life. It was now or never. The time had come for her to make her own way and work hard for her audience to finally see her for who she was rather than as the sister of her famous brother. And that there was the clincher—that would be the game changer. As soon as she found her own voice and figured out what message she wanted to deliver to her fans and the media, she'd be able to take that next step she so desperately needed for her career to finally be everything she had hoped and dreamed.

After understanding Jenni's backstory and getting to know her more, it hit me. A phrase came to mind that summed up her uniqueness to the tee: she was perfectly imperfect. That's what she had to focus on, that was the quality that would set her apart and help her connect to her audience and win them over once and for all. At the time, Pilar Montenegro was very popular—she was a singer who had a huge hit and looked like a goddess in her music videos—so one day I approached Jenni and said, "You know, Jen, there are more women like you than like Pilar Montenegro."

"What do you mean?" she asked.

"That there are a lot more women who aren't perfect, who are a little insecure, who've been through the ringer and question where they're going in life, while also comparing their physical appearance to these impossible beauty standards."

"Wow," said Jenni. "I never thought about that."

"Yeah, well that's who you need to be catering to."

Something clicked in Jen and that's when things started to evolve. As Jen and I reflected on how to newly present her, all roads seemed to organically point to urban culture. After all, Jen grew up in Long Beach with Mary J. Blige as one of her main muses and rap flow from Tupac and NWA as everyday soundtracks. Her personal connection to that sound and feeling was woven into her Mexican-American experience, birthing a completely new culture of music of which Jen was singularly poised as the mother. Since I grew up with a similar cultural experience, as a Mexican-American, I resonated with the concept from the start. We were the perfect team to bring forth a vibe and a sound that spoke directly to our specific cultural community.

It was in this newly discovered sweet spot between heritage and the here-and-now that we were able to create a unique space in which Jenni could artistically thrive. Jenni was relatable, she was perfectly imperfect, she had the potential to connect to her audience on a much more personal level, and I was hoping she would tap into this possibility.

That's when Jenni slowly became that strong, independent woman to her audience. The woman she had always been in private was now starting to shine through her songs. And you can immediately see this difference in her next album, *Simplemente la mejor*. She'd listened to my advice and really paid attention to her song selection, carefully choosing tunes that rang true to her, reflected who she was, and created a clear theme and message for her fans. She'd found her voice and was ready to share it with the world. You can also see this inner evolution in the album's imaging. She'd gone from Mexicana with a hat to urban Chicana to glam-gal Jenni Rivera. It was a clear shift in focus and the beginning of her rise to stardom. Jenni was now a woman singing to her fellow women about love, loss, lust, having fun, and what it means to be a woman. And it worked. She was finally singing from her heart and reaching the hearts of many others who were able to relate to her much more than any of the other perfect, model-like stars out there. And by opening her heart and letting the real Jenni come alive through her music, she was also connecting on a deeper level with her audience, creating a loyal fan base that would become her rock, one of the key reasons she continued to do what she did, a fan base that would always love and support her through life, death, and beyond.

In addition to connecting with women, Jenni was shattering the glass ceiling of what had been until then a male-dominated music genre: banda music. Its lyrics often described guys bragging about their womanizing ways and their wild nights out drinking. The music represented a certain brand of festive machismo that made for very male audiences. Then Jenni Rivera came along and decided to tell the other side of the story, the woman's story, her story. She turned the tables on the male banda bravado and sang it from the female point of view, calling out the no-good, cheating sons-of-bitches who came home drunk every night; condemning the assholes who bailed on their wives and kids; and demanding that women rise up and take charge of their lives. She didn't just sing about it, either—she lived it. Jenni didn't need male audience approval, because her female fans became her personal army. Banda started to move from its male-centric ideals to a celebration of female empowerment and survival.

In this way, Jenni not only captured the hearts of the Chicano audience that connected to her urban vibe, but also won over a new breed of female fans who resonated with her struggles and were inspired by her resilience. She became the pied piper for the curvy Latina who wanted a voice, for the jaded woman who couldn't find love, for the single mother who was up against the world, and for the woman who was abused, the woman who was raped, the woman who was lied to. Jenni became the voice for all of these women because she was all of these women in one, and she was basically reassuring them: "Hey, we matter too!"

Now, let me be clear. This transformation, finding her voice and making herself heard, was far from an easy feat. We'd go to radio promo runs to pitch her CD or single to the music directors, and they would take it and literally toss it in the trash right before our eyes. But Jenni kept the faith. And that inner faith that she leaned on throughout her life pushed her forward even when she had to deal with creeps who propositioned her in exchange for playing her music. "How long are you in town tonight?" they'd ask her after having thrown her music in the trash. "*Vamos a comer. Let's go have something to eat.*" And, as much as she wanted to make it in this industry, she had the balls to say no. Jen knew what she wanted and how she wanted to achieve it, and no way in hell was it going to be by sleeping her way to the top.

That was Jenni to the core. She always spoke her mind, regardless of whether it rubbed people the wrong way or made them uncomfortable, and she sure as hell didn't play into the role of the dainty little woman who bows her head down and obeys men's every wish and command. Once, during these radio promo meetings, we encountered a huge radio personality who refused to have her on the show because she was too scandalous and set a bad example for the women in the show's audience. What? We couldn't believe our ears. So Jen looked this person straight in the eye and said, "Okay, no problem. I won't go on your show now. But mark my words—one day you're going to want me back. That day will come and I'm not going to forget this." That day most definitely came. After making huge strides in her career, when she was in high demand, this person's team came a calling, begging to have her on the show, willing to do everything in their power to convince her to accept. And accept she did. While the show was taping live, the host bragged about having brought his listeners the great Jenni Rivera, a woman who fought for women, but as the interview unfolded the tension in the air rose. Jen was there, complying and playing her part, but not without taking constant jabs at this jerk every chance she had, and this time there was nothing he could do but roll with the punches. Her success had spoken for itself.

We live in a society where everyone is trying to be someone, and I think once Jen understood she didn't have to be someone she wasn't, she was finally ready to embrace her perfectly imperfect self. After all, she was a single working mother, the provider for her family, she'd had to hustle to get food on the table, her life was anything but perfect, and now it was time to be okay with that.

As soon as she embraced her perfectly imperfect self and brought it to the stage of her musical career, she really hit the jackpot. She was no longer just another rising star, she was real, she was honest. Now her fans, her army of women, were discovering that she too had gone through a teenage pregnancy, she too had suffered an abusive relationship, she too was a single mother—and not of one or two, but of five children. She was the driving force in her family, the glue that kept them all together, always working that extra mile to make sure everyone had what they needed, digging herself out of welfare and following her passions, even if that meant giving up precious time with her beloved children for life on the road to make it happen. Jenni knew that in order to be successful there were sacrifices she would have to endure. Not being at home with her kids was the biggest sacrifice she made for them. It pained her greatly to leave them and not be there for them in their day-to-day experiences, but she knew it was what she needed to do to provide for them and give them a better life. So she found her voice, she embraced her perfectly imperfectness, and she charged forward, ready to take down any obstacles in her way and make her dreams a reality.

Chapter 3

Life on the Road

 Jenni Rivera ✔
@jennirivera

"Si no me hubieran cerrado tantas puertas, no las tendria que haber tumbado a patadas...y no estaria mal de mi rodilla" ;-)

🌐 Translate from Spanish

8/16/12, 4:17 PM

166 RETWEETS **132** LIKES

When I first got on board with Jenni as her manager, I not only needed to understand what made her tick, I also had to see for myself what kind of audience she drew, who her fans were, and why they kept coming back for more. Figuring out the magic ingredient in this blossoming relationship between singer and fan would help us eventually reach more people and land gigs at bigger venues, one of Jenni's main goals, so I set off to one of her gigs back in 2003 to see what she was all about on stage.

Jenni was the opening act, something she had been doing for a while in hopes of exposing her voice and style to larger audiences. It was an uphill battle. First off, she was playing to male-dominated audiences who were there to see the male-centric banda groups who celebrated their machismo. They were not interested in some woman opening the night, and even less so one who at first glance didn't seem to have the traditional pretty-girl, model-like sex appeal they were used to seeing in other female singers. I quickly realized this would be a tough crowd to win over, and I finally understood why Jen had been so focused on doing covers. At least those were songs they recognized, a first step to getting the audience's attention. So now it all came down to delivery. And boy could Jen deliver. She belted those songs out as if she were performing on the biggest stage on earth, regardless of whether the audience was paying attention or simply passing the time till the main act came on. And that's when I noticed the Jenni Rivera phenomenon taking place before my eyes.

As soon as the women in the audience started to pick up on the lyrics Jen was singing, it was as if they were coming out of a deep slumber. They started exchanging looks, glancing her way, and paying closer attention to what she had to say. Because Jen didn't just stand on stage and sing songs, she worked the room, she interacted with her audience, and as she spoke directly to them, it was like she had woken up the wolf. Regardless of whether they were single and with their girlfriends or coupled and with their significant others, those women came alive. They edged nearer to the stage, pulled in by this singer up there, expressing thoughts that they had wanted to voice but didn't dare say out loud. And Jen was there, leading them through this awakening, her songs like battle cries and protest anthems that placed women squarely in the game. It was beautiful to watch.

So, yes, they were listening to songs they knew, but they were also discovering this brash young woman who wasn't afraid to tell it like it is. Ultimately, what won them over wasn't her voice, it wasn't the covers, it was her charisma, her personality, her charm, her balls, the fearless strength she displayed on stage in those initial, male-dominated gigs. She was suddenly becoming their pied piper, and the news was spreading like wild fire. With each consecutive gig, the audience numbers began to visibly rise, at times literally doubling from one night to the next. A few gigs later, when we looked around, we suddenly realized the room was filled with a predominantly female audience. Word was getting around that there was a badass lady on stage singing and speaking to and for women. They had to go see it for themselves, and as soon as they saw her in action, they were hooked. This is how Jen began to build her loyal fan base, one that went from ten, twenty, thirty, to hundreds, thousands, and eventually millions.

Although her fan base was undoubtedly mostly made up of women, men came flocking to her shows too. Yes, some were the husbands and boyfriends who were there accompanying their partners, but single men quickly discovered two things about Jenni's shows: she had an undeniable sex appeal, and her performances were the perfect place to pick up other single women. They knew that the odds would be in their favor, so they'd show up in hopes of making a connection, and, observing this, Jenni would outright tease them about it from the stage with her characteristic charm. Yeah, they liked her music, but, hey, let's be real, it's kind of hard to really dig a show when the person performing is basically talking shit about you the entire night. Nevertheless, they stuck it out and ended up having a great time.

When Jen realized that the audience numbers were on the up and up and her fan base was growing, I remember she reacted the same way she would react later, each time she hit a personal milestone in her career, like when she sold out the Staples Center: she was always grateful and in awe that they loved her so much and supported her no matter what—every fan was special to her. From day one to the very last day of her life, she never took them for granted; she was consistently and constantly grateful, giving them all she had because she understood from the start that her fans were the ones who helped her feed her family and allowed her to follow her passion. She'd often say, "I thank God for giving me this audience. You lift me up, cheer me on, love me. Thanks for making me happy!"

At the start of her music career, Jen didn't have the full support of a record label, she wasn't a producer's product, she was the result of hard work, perseverance, faith, and her fans' loyalty. She earned her fame and in the process she started a movement. This phenomenon set the course and built the infrastructure for the person who would later become known as La Diva de la Banda, and she finally had the right group of people in place to help her make it all come to fruition. Along with me, Jenni's team included her assistant, Jessie; her publicist, Yanalté Galván; her road manager, Gabriel Vázquez; and her four-piece Norteño band.

At first, her fans would come up to her and give her letters and small presents, from bracelets to little medals to prayer cards to keep her safe, and Jenni cherished each and every gift so much she designated a trunk in her garage just for these trinkets. She'd take the letters to her office and open and read them herself, but there came a point where there were too many for her to handle alone; that's when Jen decided she needed help, so she recruited Jessie, her bass player's wife, to help her handle the fan mail. Jessie also went on the road with Jenni and was in charge of helping her out with whatever she needed, including snapping photos and taking care of the concert merchandise. Jenni was a business woman, after all, and her keen entrepreneurial spirit never slept, so she knew that she could kill two birds with one stone by selling concert merchandise at her shows: the fans would go home happy, and she'd go home with some extra cash to continue supporting her family.

Then there was Yanalté Galván, her publicist, a short and feisty lady with a passion that bordered on bullying—exactly what Jenni needed at the start of her career. If she was going to really break through this difficult market, she needed someone as aggressive and full of gumption as Yanalté on her side. Yanalté was instrumental in getting Jen's career off the ground, a badger who would do nothing short of making sure that Jen got the publicity she needed. They later parted ways, but when I joined the team, they were going full-steam ahead, and we were all in this together. We believed in Jen and wanted to see her accomplish everything she set out to do, and we couldn't have done it without Gabriel "Gabo" Vázquez, her road manager, who shaped her touring career and road life and knew how to get her the gigs she needed to hit the ground running, so she could reach those long-awaited milestones in her career.

Gabo and Jen officially met in 2001; however, they first crossed paths in 1999 at an event in Stockton, California. Many bands were taking the stage that day, so it was a pretty hectic scene, with trails of people coming and going. Yet, Gabo recalls as if it were yesterday seeing Jen at that event, standing next to the stairs that led to the stage, dressed in black, with the mic in hand, waiting for her turn to go on, completely alone amid the sea of people and activity. It really hit him, how lonely she looked, with no one there to accompany her before her performance. Her manager was likely tracking down the promoter to get paid, who knows, but Gabo just can't shake that first image of her. There were no fans to be seen—and those events were usually swarming with them because they knew exactly where to find their favorite artists— it was just Jen and her mic against the world. Gabo was so taken aback by this desolate scene that he decided to approach her.

"Good evening."

"Good evening," she answered

"Do you need anything?" asked Gabo. *"Estamos a la orden. We're at your service."*

"Oh, no, thank you. I'm about to go on stage, but thank you."

She didn't know who Gabo was, but she was very gracious and kind in their interaction. Gabo was in the music business, so he knew she was Lupillo Rivera's sister, that godforsaken title that haunted her wherever she went. When Gabo tells this story, he is always in awe because he never in his life would've imagined that he would end up working for this woman standing before him for the following decade. He never thought this woman, who seemed somewhat abandoned and alone, known only as Lupillo's sister, would become the Diva we all grew to love, our legendary Jenni Rivera.

But back then it was all about Lupillo. Gabo had heard one of Jenni's songs on the radio, but he wasn't a big fan of her voice, which was still somewhat thin and jarring. And he thought,

Lupillo Rivera, now Jenni Rivera, who's next? Their children and grandchildren? What are they, the Jackson 5? Nevertheless, when a friend in common, popular L.A. radio host Gerardo "El Carnalillo" Tello, reached out to Gabo and told him Jenni was looking for him, Gabo gave him the greenlight to give her his phone number.

At the time, Gabo was doing well for himself, working with different bands, including Palomo, who had a hit, "No me conoces aún," that had been number one on the Billboard charts for weeks, so work was thriving. Jenni had taken note of two successful events, one for Pablo Montero and the other for Palomo, that had happened recently, and when she asked her friend "El Carnalillo" who had brought these groups to California, he mentioned Gabo. He told her Gabo had his own office and was doing very well for himself, so she asked to meet him. Gabo wasn't sure why she wanted to talk to him; he figured she had her father's team at her disposal, the same one that was taking care of Lupillo, so he was curious to see what she had to say.

The following day, as Gabo checked his messages in his office—cell phones were a hot commodity, but the minutes could run up quite a bill, so landlines were still a solid form of communication—there was one from Jenni introducing herself in her polite and well-spoken manner, asking for an appointment to meet. Gabo was impressed by the message, so he called her back immediately. They exchanged greetings and, much like she did with me when we meet a couple of years later, she cut right to the chase. "I'm desperate, I feel my talent is going to waste." Gabo recalls that phrase, "going to waste" or "*desaprovechada*," as if it were yesterday because she kept repeating it over and over in that first conversation.

"I've been working with my brother Lupillo Rivera's team, but it seems they only have time for him. I'm ready to work hard and make something of myself in this industry. That's why I'm calling you."

"What do you expect from all of this? Do you see this as a temporary or lifelong career?" asked Gabo. He'd heard through the industry grapevine that she had just had her fifth child, so he was testing the waters to make sure she was for real.

"My career is very important to me," she said. "I want to sing and be remembered like Paquita la del Barrio."

She had a clear vision of where she wanted to go and what she wanted to accomplish. Gabo quickly realized that Jenni was in it for the long haul, she felt she had a future in this, and she was in it to succeed. Her entrepreneurial spirit kicked in later, but when she spoke to Gabo, all she wanted to do was sing. She knew she needed more exposure and that's where Gabo came in. Once he heard her conviction and how hard she was willing to work, he was in.

When they started working together, Jen was still playing small local clubs and wasn't reaching as many people as she needed in order to survive in this industry. She had an underground following, but in order to get booked in bigger venues, she needed a bigger fan base. Gabo figured that the best way to do this was to book her as an opening act for groups that played for larger crowds. That's when she started playing more of those bigger male-dominated circuits and slowly began to win over her army of women through her performances.

Meanwhile, by the time Jen teamed up with Gabo, she and her husband, Juan Lopez, had quit their day jobs to dedicate all their time to her career. Juan had taken on the role as her manager, which in the end did not bode well for their relationship, especially since, early on in their marriage, Jen had gotten wind that Juan had been cheating on her with other women from his office. A few years later, she sat me down and told me the story of how she handled it, and I couldn't believe my ears.

Juan was a good-looking man who was a great father to Jenni's children. He seemed like everything Jenni had been looking for in a partner: a man who was a good father, handsome, loved her, and smelled amazing all the time (a remark she often made about him). But he was lacking the work ethic her father had instilled in her from a young age. When they quit their jobs to focus on her career, she became the sole provider of the house. Yes, he made money, but she was the one paying him, so technically it was still money she earned. She put in endless hours to get her career off the ground while he stayed home taking long baths with *pepinos* on his eyes and a face mask, more focused on his looks than his job. Suddenly, she started to feel like she was the man in the relationship, something she did not enjoy one bit. Yeah, he bought her gifts and all, but even though the thought counted, it was hard for her to accept them because she knew they were purchased with her own money—like the time when he gave her an expensive fur coat and her initial response was, "Oh, great, so my money bought me a fur coat." However, before she had decided to sideline everything and give her music career a real chance, her marriage to Juan suffered the ultimate challenge: betrayal.

In June 1998 Jen found out Juan was having an affair with a few women at his office; however, instead of exploding a la Jenni, she held it all in and said nothing. She carefully planned her revenge and put it in action, spending the following two months getting back in shape and winning him over, making him fall in love with her all over again, acting like the perfect wife. Things were apparently going better for them, but little did Juan know this was all part of Jen's plan. It all went down one August morning in 1998, after making love to him the way he liked it the night before, then waking up and making him his favorite breakfast. As he sat there basking in how good he had it, telling her he loved her, she smiled, gave him his lunch, and kissed him good-bye. However, later that morning she had her friend drive her to his office, where she stormed in and confronted him with the affairs, humiliating him in front of his coworkers and telling him it was over. But the plan wasn't completely over and done with yet. Jen had recently seen *Waiting to Exhale*, which proved to be just the inspiration she needed for what came next. She drove back home, grabbed all his precious belongings, and burned all his shit in their driveway. As she told me all of this, it felt like it was straight out of a movie. "You're one dangerous and crazy woman," I said to her. That seemed like the end, but it wasn't.

A year later, he came crawling back, and she took him in, hoping they'd have it better this second time around. They already had their daughter, Jenicka, who was born in 1997 (a year before she pulled the *Waiting to Exhale* on him), and as they were trying to make things work, she became pregnant with their second child, her fifth, Johnny, who was born in 2001. And that's where Gabo comes into the picture as road manager. He had no idea what he was walking into, and he was caught right in the middle of their crossfire the first week on the job, on their first promo tour to Miami.

Telemundo had invited Jenni, tickets and all, to Miami to appear on one of their morning shows. Gabo, Jenni, and Juan arrived at the Miami hotel the night before the show, checked into their rooms, and went straight to bed. It was already late and they had to be up bright and early the next day. They agreed to meet in the hotel lobby the following morning at 7:00 a.m., with enough time to have a quick breakfast or coffee and hop in the scheduled car that would be picking them up from the channel and driving them to the show.

So, that next morning, at 7:00 a.m. sharp, Gabo was standing in the lobby waiting for Jenni and Juan to come down. He'd served himself a cup of tea and continued to patiently wait as the minutes ticked by. At around 7:20 a.m., the elevator doors slid open and out stormed Jenni, somewhat disheveled and late. Gabo told me later that he had pictured the two of them coming down together, hand-in-hand, ready for the show and their morning cup of joe—he had no idea what he was in for. Jen beelined over to Gabo, pleading, "Gabo, help me, please, this man is going to destroy my things, please!" In that instant, the other elevator opened its doors and out came Juan, trying to catch up with her, wearing shorts and a shirt—also not ready for the show. Gabo didn't know what to do. He just kept looking at Jen, then at Juan, in hopes that they would resolve this issue without involving him. Again, he was pretty new to the team, and now he was suddenly smack in the middle of this couple's fight. She continued to plead for my help, afraid that he would burn all her stuff, just like she had done a couple of years earlier, but Gabo didn't know where this fear stemmed from, he didn't know the story, so he was completely taken aback.

Meanwhile, the car that was scheduled to pick them up had already arrived, so Gabo had to figure out a way to take control of this scene in the lobby and get Jenni to her scheduled interview

ASAP. Jenni realized the car was there and they were already late, so she asked Gabo again, "Please help me. I'll be fine on my own at the channel. You can catch up with me later, but please stay and make sure he doesn't destroy any of my stuff."

Gabo later told me, "I saw how anxious and distressed she was, but I also thought that if I agreed with her, Juan might get angry at me. I didn't know him that well yet, since it was our first trip together. For a second I even thought, *Is this a joke? Are they playing a prank on me or what?* I just didn't know what to do. Out of all the scenarios I've had to deal with on the road, this was a first, and most definitely not the last. I later learned that these explosive fights were normal between them, but I sure wish I had known back then in Miami!"

Gabo finally agreed, calling the producer to make sure everything was set up right for Jenni and explaining that he had gotten "held up" and would arrive later. She grabbed her stuff and took off to Telemundo, while he stayed behind to face the remnants of their latest fight, not knowing how Juan would react and what he would have to do to take control of the situation.

"*Pinche vieja*, she's *loca*!" said Juan as soon as Jenni was out of earshot. "She got angry about another woman, but I told her over and over again that nothing had happened, that I hadn't done anything." Juan went on to tell him they'd thrown things at each other, a hair straightener, whatever they could get their hands on—something that was common in their fights. Things always flew through the air when their arguments got heated. Gabo, flabbergasted by the whole situation, was finally able to reason with Juan, reminding him that this was the first day of a week-long promo trip that ended with them flying straight to one of

Jenni's Friday night gigs. So Juan calmed down, and promised he wouldn't do anything to her stuff. Crisis averted! One down, many more to go.

Life on the road with Jenni was always entertaining, to say the least. Gabo has fond memories of those early days, where they would all pile into a conversion van with seats that turned into beds, and hit the highway, touring every weekend and many weekdays, playing the circuits, trying to make Jenni Rivera a household name. Juan would drive, she'd sit next to him, and Gabo would sit in the back with the musicians. Jen had put together a four-piece Norteño band that became her musical entourage.

Yes, she recorded banda-style, with many more musicians, but early on it was more cost-effective for her to perform with a smaller Norteño band. This was a big step for her; it meant she was no longer working with local musicians in each town, but instead rocking out with a self-curated crew of guys there to back La Diva's act. Two of them were her friends: El Gordo, the music director, and Gil, the band leader. They were really talented and they knew Jen like the back of their hand. She traveled, toured, lived, and created with these men. The other two musicians rotated because in the beginning there weren't enough steady gigs to keep them all on full-time.

El Gordo and Gil stayed on with Jenni until around the *Parrandera, rebelde y atrevida* album released in 2005. After that we went full banda. To Gabo's credit, he was the one who told her: "If you want to charge more money, you have to get your own banda. The only way you're going to get more money is performing with banda." And it was hard. She saved money with the Norteño band, so it was tough to decide to go out on a limb and increase her overhead, but it paid off. From then on, she'd still use el Gordo when she was recording. He'd come around to guide her when she was laying down the vocal tracks. Yet, by then, Jen didn't really need much guidance in that area. I think she kept accepting his help to keep him in the loop in her career. Jenni was such a loyal person that if you were loyal to her, she found a way for you to stay on board. She never forgot the people who were there for her when she was a nobody. That was Jenni for you.

In any case, back on the road, Jen was usually the lone woman in that crew, but she knew how to handle herself. From the start, Jen always made it clear she was one of the guys. She grew up in a house with four brothers, her little sister came later, so getting down with the fellas was nothing new to her, even now when she was in the thick of it, getting hot-boxed in the tour van by a gaggle of burly musicians; the kind of dudes who always had a beer in one hand and a joint in the other. It was an experience of growth for her, not because she was the only woman, but because she was the leader. It wasn't about being a woman; it was about being the boss.

Later, Jen hired Jessie, the bass player's wife, as her assistant, and she'd also join them on the road, selling merchandise and photos to the growing number of fans. As Gabo recalls, "We were all pulling our weight to help her make it. I remember we'd make pit stops at an ampm or a 7-Eleven before hitting the freeway to load up the van with food for the drive, which usually was around four to five hours long between stops. We'd get lots of junk food, Doritos, Fritos, Gatorade, peanuts, water too. A typical weekend meant driving to Bakersfield on Friday, San José on Saturday, and Fresno or Stockton on Sunday, then back to L.A. Later, once we started expanding our territory and getting out-of-state gigs, we'd drive, in that same van, to Arizona, Nevada, Oregon, and Washington."

Juan was only around for the beginning of these road trips—their relationship had come to an end by the time Jen started touring more frequently. She knew that being married to her so-called manager would be difficult, especially to a good-looking man who was in the audience doing his thing, getting attention from the crowd, while she was on stage seeing what she felt was his flirtatiousness in all its glory. And, given their history, her jealousy was far from unfounded, and incredibly difficult to manage while performing.

One time, Gabo recalls, they had traveled to San Antonio, Texas, for a gig, and her jealousy suddenly spun out of control when he least expected it. Jenni was on stage performing, doing a fantastic job as always, the crowd cheering her on and loving every minute of it, when Juan turned to Gabo and said, "I'll be right back. I'm going to the bathroom." He walked off, and along the way a young woman stopped him to ask him something about Jenni, at least that was Juan's version of the story. Gabo didn't even realize what was happening until seconds later, when he heard Jenni say over the mic, "*Te estoy viendo cabrón, te estoy viendo …*" (I see you, *cabrón*, I see you.) Some people in the audience started looking over their shoulders trying to figure out what the hell she was talking about because it had nothing to do with the song she was singing; it came totally out of left field.

Before Gabo had the chance to even react, he heard her say, "*Ahorita vengo. Espérenme.*" (Hold on, I'll be right back.) And she stopped singing midway through a tune, set the mic down, and left the stage while the band continued to play, glancing at one another and wondering what Jenni was up to now.

She stomped down those stairs, flew by Gabo, and headed straight to Juan, who was still chatting with this woman, clueless as to what had just happened behind him. And, man, did she go in on him, "What do you think you're doing, *pendejo*? Do you think I'm blind? Do you think for one second that I can't see who you're looking at? I've got eyes everywhere! Just wait until we get back to the hotel! All hell's gonna break loose!" Juan was taken so aback he was speechless. Gabo remembers, "As soon as I realized what was happening, I ran after Jenni. She had left the stage midway through a song and had to go back and finish it! It was only a matter of minutes, and as I reached her, she was already wrapping it up and heading back to her performance, but I never knew how those situations were going to unfold and how long they could take." Thankfully, after she gave Juan a piece of her mind, she whirled around, got back on stage, finished the damn song, and continued her show as if nothing had happened. "I really don't think Juan would be so shameless as to do something like that right under Jenni's nose," says Gabo, "but when there are infidelities and jealousy, all bets are off."

When Jenni left Juan, she hired a driver who took Juan's place on the tours and helped her with whatever she needed. Things went smoother for Gabo after that because this guy had taken Jenni's husband's role on the road, but she didn't sleep with him, so there was no damn drama to be had. That's when Jenni and Gabo really began to bond and forge their friendship.

During those long journeys, they began to open up to each other, beyond work-related subjects, getting into more personal stuff, until eventually they became as close as siblings. When work was done for the day or night, they'd all share some beers or a few tequilas and tell jokes, rolling over with laughter. Then Jenni's smile would suddenly morph into a weeping willow, and she'd wail out, "I miss my husband!" then add between sobs, "I miss my kids!" Gabo, now used to these sudden outbursts of emotion, would respond, "Relax, *mija*, don't worry, you'll get to see them in about a day." Jen was hoping she could fix things with Juan, but it was too late. Too much water under the bridge. Until one day she finally said, "I can't take it anymore," and it was over for good. That's around the same time she started pouring her emotions into her performances, shedding tears on stage, overwhelmed by the pain caused by the end of her second marriage and the time she had to be away from her children.

Jen was always incredibly open and clear with her children about what she was doing and why she had to leave them to go on the road. Although she sheltered them, she was always straight forward and honest with them. They knew what mama was doing. They understood that when she wasn't with them, it was because she was out working for them, for their needs, to give them better lives, so they never lacked anything … but that didn't mean it hurt her any less. It was a huge sacrifice for her, the biggest one she had to make; it really killed her inside, but it was all for them, for her princesses and princes, for the real loves of her life.

Before Jenni passed, during one of our many conversations on this topic, she expressed that all she really wanted was to be close to her children, to not miss any more birthdays, to be there for their school events, to be nearby when they needed her the most.

And I said, "Look at Shakira. She was incredibly successful, even managed to cross over into the American market, but once she got married and had children, she put her career on hold to be with her family." I pointed out to Jen that she had done the opposite. She had started off as a mom and then decided to work hard on her career for her kids. It was most definitely a motherly act, just not the traditional stay-at-home kind, and it had worked. She'd made it work. Even when she was traveling, she always did everything in her power to loop in her children, to call them between gigs and check up on them, to incorporate them as much as possible into her busy life. She was a mom who had to go on the road to make a living, but a mama bear nonetheless.

While she struggled with these separations, Gabo struggled to get her gigs, especially when he first joined her team. "It was really hard at the beginning," he recalls. "I'd try to sell her to the concert promoters I knew, but they just wanted Lupillo. They thought hiring Jenni was a waste of time and money. And I'd insist that she had her Malandrinas, her army of women who faithfully followed her everywhere. They were still hesitant, so I'd say, 'Listen, give her a shot, and if it turns out you're not happy, just don't book her again.' Slowly, I was able to convince them to give us a shot—having a good relationship with them from before also helped." That's how Gabo managed to pull it off.

The promoters agreed to book her for a very low initial fee that was tied to the crowd she drew. The more people she brought, the better paid the gig would be. The ladder ahead to stardom was a long one, but they had at least gone up the first few steps. However, absolutely nothing happened overnight. It took a lot of hard work, rejection, convincing those who were skeptical, but in the end, we did it. Think about it: if it's hard for men to break into this music scene, imagine how hard it is for a woman? As Gabo said in one of our conversations, "The problem with female artists in Mexican Regional music is that usually they look great on the venue's billboard, but they don't sell tickets. Why? Because women fans are very, very jealous. They don't want to take their husbands to see a woman who's hotter than them. They may listen to their songs, but they sure as hell don't flock to their concerts. Now with Jenni it was different. She didn't look like a model, she looked like them, and she was singing to and for them with her characteristic spunk and charisma. She wasn't a threat, she was their best gal pal, she was their ally, she was their champion. Jenni could sell the hell out of those tickets, and I knew it. Now I just had to convince the promoters to give her a shot."

Eventually, she started getting more and more airplay, and suddenly it was the promoters who were knocking on our door asking her to please play at their venues. Women didn't really have a voice in the Mexican Regional music genre until Jen came along. And with time, and hard work, her growing number of fans helped Jen begin to see herself in this new light. With each show, she noticed the huge impact she had on her audience, and this only pushed her to give them more and more of herself. She'd often say, "I have to do my best in every show, no matter how large or small, as if it were the first, as if it were the last." And that's exactly what she did. No matter what stage she was on, she always gave it her all, even if that meant breaking down and weeping onstage because the line between the expression of her art and her personal life was a fine one. The more she performed, the more people wanted to know the details of her life story, and right out of the gate, she was an open book.

Chapter 4

Love and Music

Jenni Rivera ✓
@jennirivera

"Ayyyy PELON!!"...

12/3/12, 9:09 PM

1,631 RETWEETS **1,207** LIKES

↩   ↻   ♥   •••

Every time Jenni hit the stage there was a transformation. As soon as she grabbed the mic, she tuned out reality and tuned in a different world. This was a world where she was in charge, where she could express her musical gift openly; it was also a shelter from her problems, a place where all she felt was the love of her fans and the exhilaration of her performance. The stage served as her respite, and in those few hours up there she could breathe and laugh and let go of whatever might have been weighing her down. There were no responsibilities; it was a place to express her emotions to the point of tears and laughter and just have a good old time. No one had the power to interrupt her during those moments on stage. However, as soon as she stepped out of the limelight, she walked right back into her reality, which was centered around her divorce from Juan López when I joined her team.

Jenni's Second Marriage to Juan López Ends in Divorce

Jenni filed for divorce in April 2003, right around the time I started working with her, so this was my first Jenni Rivera media wrangle. The divorce in itself was difficult because her two youngest children, Jenicka and Johnny, loved their dad, and she didn't want her problems with him to affect the relationship they had with Juan. It was also difficult on Jenni because she had worked so hard trying to make it work for her kids, for herself. Juan was a good-looking man and a bad ass who didn't take shit from anyone, the kind of man Jen imagined would keep her safe. Yet, as the years went by, things took a turn for the worse in their relationship, and they were going nowhere fast. Their fights escalated, as did Jen's frustration for feeling that she was the man of the house, the provider, the ambitious one, the one who rolled up her sleeves and did whatever it took to get the job done. Yes, Juan was her manager, but it was difficult; there wasn't a clear line between what he made and what she brought home, so that became another constant struggle. And then there were his infidelities, which only made the situation worse. Jen's jealousy skyrocketed after discovering his first affairs, and she was never capable of fully trusting him again. So while her music career was finally beginning to go somewhere, her marriage was tanking, and all roads led to their inevitable divorce.

Up until here, it sounds like the familiar divorce story we've all heard time and again, infidelities, irreconcilable differences, and so on, but then Juan threw in a curve ball that sent Jen reeling. Juan not only was requesting alimony, he wanted to include a sunset clause in his spousal payment so that he would continue receiving a percentage of her earnings throughout the duration of her career. How could this strong macho man suddenly turn around and ask for alimony? This was unheard of among the Mexicanos we knew, but what really set her off was that he was also suddenly claiming ownership of her career. She was shocked and furious, "I can't believe the son of a bitch has the balls to even ask me for this," she said to me. "I'm raising the kids, taking care of everything, I stood by him when he went to jail, I married him so he wouldn't get deported, I had to deal with his infidelities, and now he has the audacity to claim to have ownership of my career?"

Yes, that's exactly what he was doing. He believed he was owed a lifelong residual from her because he claimed he had initiated and invested in her career. Boy did that light Jenni on fire. No one made her. She made herself. But he had been afforded a certain lifestyle under Jenni's wing, and now he felt he was entitled to keep it. He'd gotten used to living comfortably and being pampered, and he wasn't about to give all that up without battling it out. But he picked a fight with the wrong woman. Jen had a huge issue with people when they suddenly felt a sense of entitlement. She'd earned every penny in her name through blood, sweat, and tears, and she believed everyone around her—employees, friends, and family—should do the same. You get out there, give it your all, and earn your spot on a team in this world. It's not simply handed over to you. Jen never received any handouts, and she'd be damned if she was about to give one to this guy.

The divorce, which Jen hoped would be a quiet one that would resolve within a year, turned into a long and arduous public battle that lasted three years and was finally settled in June 2006. My initial approach was to control what went public, to carefully decide what we shared with the media, but Jen had another idea in mind: she wanted to use the media to give light to her battle, something that I believed to be very risky. The media is like a snake. You have to be very careful with how you handle it because it could just as easily swing around and bite and poison you when you least expect it. That's pretty much how I put it to Jen when we were going back and forth on how public to go with this divorce, but Yanalté, her then publicist, who thrived on garnering attention for her regardless of whether it was positive or negative press, didn't agree with me and continued to fuel Jenni's fire, one that was easy to feed.

Jen was a sensitive soul who didn't really think things through when she was hurt, but rather immediately reacted with her emotions. She'd raise her guard and slide into attack mode, throwing punches left and right until she knocked down the culprit. If something didn't sit well with Jen, she wouldn't take her time to figure out the best way to handle the situation. She'd pick up a phone, go to a TV show, open up Twitter, and openly confront whoever had rubbed her the wrong way, so my reasonable approach on how to handle the media quickly went out the window this first time around. It wasn't until later in life that she learned how to first process information and then react accordingly, but it was never in her nature. It went against her very essence, and it always required a huge effort on her behalf not to pounce like a tiger when feeling threatened.

In the end, she'd had to pay spousal support while the divorce proceedings unfolded, until the judge on their family court case finally ruled in her favor in June 2006. She only had to pay his attorney fees and would no longer be responsible for his alimony. Once Juan stopped receiving his monthly check from her, he quickly realized he could no longer afford his current lifestyle, so he turned to drug trafficking to make ends meet, and a year later, in October 2007, he was caught and sentenced to ten years in prison.

By then, Jen had made amends with Juan, for their children's sake. During the divorce proceedings, she tried to keep a fair balance, fighting for what was rightfully hers without tarnishing the image of her children's father in their presence. In truth, he had always been a great father to their two children, and Jenni wanted to encourage them to continue having a relationship with him. It wasn't easy, but Jen was very upfront and honest with her kids, so when she filed for divorce, she sat them down and said, "I'm getting divorced. He's still your daddy and a great one at that. Mommy loves him, but we can't be together." Simple and to the point, that was always her approach with her children. And she kept her word.

She did everything in her power to not allow the animosity and disappointment she felt toward Juan during the divorce affect the kids and the relationship they had with their father. Even when their lawyers were battling out head to head, and she was seething inside at his audacity and entitlement, she would still keep it civil and greet him with a kiss on the cheek in front of the kids to give them some sense of a family unity. And a year later, when Juan was arrested, convicted, and sentenced to prison, Jen herself would drive her kids to see their dad in jail. It wasn't a nanny, a grandma, an aunt, it was Jen. She didn't care that she was a rising star and people recognized her in that waiting room; she simply embraced the situation and did what needed to be done. Why? For her kids. They were the reason and motivation behind everything she did and accomplished in her life.

Meanwhile, while dealing with this ugly divorce, Jen was falling for someone new, the man who would eventually become her soul mate, her greatest love and best friend till the day she left this earth.

Shortly after joining Jen's team, aside from putting me up to speed with her career and her divorce, she also mentioned she had recently met someone and was smitten. His name was Fernando. He worked in the promotions department at Que Buena, a local radio station, and helped set up events for the station's marketing and promotions department. Jen crossed paths with him at a "meet and greet" Que Buena hosted for her at a shoe warehouse in April 2003. Aside from setting up the event, Fernando also had to take care of her, escorting her to the holding area before she met the fans and making sure she had everything she needed. They hit it off instantly.

Fernando was a handsome Mexicano, younger than Jen, and rough around the edges. On the other hand, Jen was very flirtatious, often making men feel awkward with her straightforward ways. She tended to be the aggressor, and many men didn't know how to handle this; they were often intimidated and speechless in her presence. This made her toy with them even further; however, if the guy she was flirting with was sharp enough to take control of the situation and flirt right back with no qualms, that definitely made her stop in her tracks and pay closer attention. And Fernando was that guy.

They didn't start dating right then and there. She was just beginning her divorce proceedings, and it was getting uglier by the minute, so her mind was elsewhere. Sometime in July, they ran into each other again, finally went on their first date, and started officially dating in August 2003. I can remember her face as if it were yesterday. Every time she spoke about him, she acted like a high school girl with butterflies in her stomach, giggling as she shared their adventures and how he made her feel. It was beautiful to witness. After being knocked down so many times, it was wonderful to see her genuinely happy and in love, but as her manager I had other concerns.

Since we were amid such a public divorce battle, it was crucial that we keep this budding romance private. If news got out that Jen was seeing someone, it could be used against her in the divorce. This wasn't easy, because Jen wore her heart on her sleeve and was so head over heels about this guy that she wanted to share it with the world—that type of chemistry and connection doesn't come around every day. It was definitely a challenge for her and for us, but we managed. What also bode well for us was Fernando himself. He wasn't into Jenni because of her rising celebrity status. He actually shunned the public eye, he wanted nothing to do with it, so keeping their relationship under wraps for a while was fine by him. If he would've been a media hog, I'd be telling quite a different story, but this man really loved Jen and was with her for the right reasons. Ferni was the kind of guy who would ride a bike or take a bus just to see Jen. He'd insist on paying for dinner, even when she was making much more than him, and at the height of her career, while he was working regular jobs, hearing her on the radio would bring a huge smile to his face.

This was Jenni's infamous *pelón*, a word she tenderly used to describe this simple, regular, baldheaded guy who made her feel like a real woman. He taught her that she was attractive and sexy just the way she was, and he showed her a carefree and fresh side of love and life that she had never experienced before. It was magical. Fernando was the liberator in her life. Jen hadn't had the chance to live her adolescence in all its glory because she had gotten pregnant at fifteen and had had to grow up and become a responsible adult, wife, and mother in a matter of months. Then she suffered abuse at the hands of Trino. She finally left him, after having three children, only to marry Juan, have two more kids, and continue adding on more responsibilities as well as financial and personal struggles. So she'd never had the chance to really let loose. She'd never gotten drunk, she'd never smoked a joint, and she hadn't had the chance to come of age sexually either. Enter Fernando. He changed all that. Not only did he allow her to experience those careless teenage years, he didn't give a shit about her growing celebrity status. "You're my girl, and that's all that matters"—that was his attitude toward Jen; it was just what she needed. He was the high school crush she had never had a chance to have.

As time went by, their relationship flourished and they fell deeper in love. It wasn't about lust, it wasn't about work, it wasn't to fulfill a need; what kept them going was an everlasting, profound, and connected friendship. That was their secret. They were soul mates, I'm sure of it. And their love for each other was as passionate as their fights, because when these two went at it, hell, they were worse than Ike and Tina.

One night, a couple of years into their relationship, I remember I got a call from Jen at 1:00 a.m. asking if I could go pick her up at Ferni's house because they'd just had a big argument. I hopped in my car and drove over, not knowing what to expect, only to arrive and find her outside in her white Adidas sweat suit smeared in grass stains. *What the hell?* I thought as I got out of the car. They were like two high school kids going at it, and I had the role of Jen's big brother. "Jen, come on, get in the car. Let's go!"

Now, remember, Jen was a grown-ass woman who already had made a name for herself in the music industry and media, and I had to make sure her image wasn't tarnished by this childish behavior. Once we were in the car, I scolded her, "What the hell were you thinking? What are you doing?" She brushed me off with some lame excuse, but scenes like this one usually boiled down to one issue: jealousy. When Jen met Fernando she was fresh off of the relationship with Juan, where she'd suffered infidelities that had awakened her jealous rage. And here was Ferni, a handsome man who was younger than her, and although he chose to be with her, that didn't stop Jen from flipping out and going at him on distrustful rants. But she wasn't the only one.

Ferni would suddenly react with extreme jealousy when she least expected it too. A match made in heaven … or hell, depending on the moment and mood. One time, Ferni showed up at a TV station where he knew Jen would be recording a show, and stood outside, threatening anyone who got in his way. He needed to see Jenni. He acted so crazy that everyone was terrified. Even her security detail didn't know what to do with him. Already used to these types of passionate scenes, Jen turned to me and said, "Pete, Fernando is outside causing a big commotion.

Can you go talk to him?" She knew that I was one of the few people who could calm him down. So I'd stroll outside and say, "Hey, Fernando, what's up? We're working, man." And I'd find a way to talk him down and reason with him, explaining that this was important for Jenni's career and asking that he put himself in her shoes for a minute. "You wouldn't want someone showing up at your job and stirring up trouble, would you?" He finally got it and left. However, only a few hours later, they would be together again, happy little lovebirds prancing around hand-in-hand as if nothing had happened. Their love always won in the end.

The desire and passion they shared for each other was with her every step of the way, regardless of whether they were together or not. This was the famous "Pelón" she often referred to on stage, the one she cried for, the one she sang for, her musical muse. As Jen's career took off, Ferni was her witness, standing by her side, daydreaming with her, never moved by how popular she was becoming, but always inspiring her and edging her on musically. He'd show her different songs, sing oldies to her, give her suggestions, share insight, and also opened her up to different music genres. He was a guy who encompassed creativity and inspired Jen to make better song and image choices along the way, and they shared a deep love and respect for music.

Jen could get down with a Norteño or Banda group just as much as she could rap her ass off—even though her rapping skills left much to be desired—to Tupac songs. She also loved R&B and Beyoncé, to the point where once I stopped by her house for a meeting and found her exercising on her treadmill in sweats and high heels! "Girl, what are you doing?" I asked her. "Oh, I heard Beyoncé does this to keep a firm butt. She says it's good for your calves too," and she kept at it. You couldn't help but smile during these moments. She was definitely a West Coast girl with West Coast influences, but she had a diverse taste in music. She was just as much a fan of Carrie Underwood—I will never forget how excited she was when she found out she was going to meet her!—as she was of Chayito Valdez and Lupita D'Alessio, and don't even get her started on Marisela and Joan Sebastián, the latter a prolific songwriter and performer whom she looked up to as one of her heavier influences throughout her music career. What she listened to depended on what she was going through at the time. Music was the soundtrack to her life.

Once she began to explore more music genres and ideas with Fernando, her musical muse, once she had her own team in place, once she understood the message she wanted to share with her audience, the one that rang true to both their life stories and her own, Jen began making better decisions, and Jenni Rivera, the artist we grew to know and love, began to take shape before our eyes.

After *Homenaje a las grandes*, there was a shift in Jenni's song selection. She now had a clear message she wanted to share with her audience, so it all came down to the songs she chose to perform. Fernando helped with on-point suggestions because he knew Jenni's heart and soul, and she also began to do her due diligence in the process. When she started making a name for herself in the industry, a lot of people, including songwriters, began to pitch her songs in hopes that she'd choose one and make it one of her future hits. But she was pickier now. She wanted to stay true to who she was, so if the lyrics didn't move her, if she couldn't relate to them in any way, then she'd simply pass them up, even if they were fantastic tunes. She was offered hits that would've probably debuted at the top of the charts, but if they didn't ring true to her, she would still say no, and had no regrets later. She just knew she couldn't do it because if she couldn't connect to the song, she wouldn't be able to give it her signature emotional performance, and that would be a disservice to her and her fans.

For the following albums, the process began to change. Jen was more self-assured and therefore much more hands on. We'd sit down and she'd tell us where she wanted to go with her next album, then we'd brainstorm and hash out the concept till we had come up with a clear theme and message. After this, Jen would handpick each song and get to work. Many of the songs were covers that she now knew how to make her own, but she liked to include a few originals as well to drive home the album's theme. Some of these originals were written for her and arrived ready for her to record, while others had a structure she liked, so she'd work with them and fine-tune the lyrics to fit her story. She also enjoyed taking a crack at writing one or two songs herself. But it wasn't like she'd wake up and sit at a studio and allot time to create these tunes; no, Jen was always on the go, so her writing process happened on the go too, usually with her planner in hand.

Yeah, Jen was old-school when it came to technology. Even when online calendars and planners became all the rage, she'd still run around town with her planner and pen in hand. That's where she jotted everything down, from appointments to meetings to lyrics to ideas for her own book, I'm talking ev-ery-thing. She did not leave home without that little tattered book. Those planners were her life, and as such, she always made sure to have backups. Much like an external hard drive in which you back up all your computer files, Jen had her assistant add all the information in her planner to two other backup planners. This way, if Jen lost one along the way, left it at a meeting, forgot it at an event, she'd always have a backup planner to take its place—not very practical but absolutely necessary, as Jen was notorious for leaving them behind. And that's where her original songs were born.

When the time came to record these babies, Jen was all business. She wasn't the type of artist who enjoys living in the studio, experimenting, trying out new things, developing songs in the moment. On the contrary, she walked into the studio only when it was time for her to lay down the vocal tracks. The actual music was usually recorded in Mazatlán, Sinaloa, by a group of banda musicians. Once they were done, those files were sent back to the L.A. studio and prepped for Jen's final magical touch. When Jen set foot in the studio, she was prepared to get the job done. She knew exactly what she wanted, so she'd listen to the music, give the producer feedback if she felt anything needed to be tweaked, and then walked into the sound booth and belted it all out in one fell swoop.

Jen knew what needed to get done and she did it. And mind you, early on, it wasn't so much about her voice but rather about her delivery. I've said it before and I'll say it again, when she began her singing career, her voice really wasn't all that; it was too tinny; it lacked depth. The voice is a musical instrument, and as such, it requires fine-tuning and practice to get it to where it needs to be. Jen had the basics, she sang in tune and had rhythm, so she had the potential to master this craft, and she was willing to put in the work to make it happen. However, she didn't have time or money to go to vocal coaches or music classes, so her classroom became the stage. She was gigging so much—one year she played three hundred venues!—that she used each two-hour show to practice, perfect, and master her craft. And on the side she smoked cigars. Why? Because she'd read somewhere that they could help mature her vocals, and she really wanted to get that raspier and fuller range down pat. She was eager to hit that vocal sweet spot. I'm not sure if it was the cigars or simply all the experience on stage, but eventually she got there, and by the end of her life and career she had become a vocal monster, with an amazing voice that moved her audience to cheers and tears.

The next step was her imaging. When I first joined Jen's team, she was slowly starting to come into her own, ditching the cowboy hat and reclaiming her roots. She was literally turning into a gorgeous butterfly before our eyes. With the help of Fernando and the way he loved and cherished her, she learned to accept and love her body. She discovered she was sexy and began to own it, and that came through in the way she presented herself on stage and on her album covers. Gone were the days of the cowboy hats. Now it was all about incorporating her West Coast influences, and it started with the iconic fedora.

Jen's signature fedora made its first appearance at a car show in Long Beach. Mexican Regional bands were usually booked at rodeos, not car shows, so Jen wasn't sure what to wear for this lowrider-loving Chicano crowd. She wanted something that would help her connect to her audience, so I put her in touch with a friend who owned a pachuco-style clothing store and was willing to sponsor a customized outfit just for the occasion. When she received it, she wasn't too happy when she realized it came with a hat. She'd recently stopped using cowboy hats and wasn't keen on putting another one on for a show, but I urged her to give it a try, and she did. Next thing I knew, she was rocking it at photo shoots and other gigs. She fell in love with the look because she felt it was unique and it helped represent her mixed heritage, balancing both her Mexican and American worlds. It was a perfect example of who she was and why she was so authentic. She was reaching out to people like me, who some call Pochos, born on this side of the border, but equally proud of our Mexican heritage.

Jen became our flag bearer; she was the first person we could fully identify with because she spoke our language. And that can clearly be seen in her video of "Amiga si lo ves." That was the first Latino video shot by Jessy Terrero, a Domincan music video director who was working with all the East Coast rappers at the time, had just wrapped a 50 Cent video, and was looking to break into the Latino market. It was fantastic; she looked amazing. That was also the first video where Jenni broke from tradition. If you watch the video and mute the music, you'll be able to focus on the imaging and fully grasp how we had managed to perfect the combination of these two worlds, which also represented Jen to the tee. She never put on an act, that was what she looked like in real life, that was her.

And her genuineness was reflected even better on stage. She was an amazing communicator, and that's what made her music so compelling and moving. She internalized each and every lyric so that when she sang about heartbreak or sorrow, she usually had someone specific in mind. She channeled her emotions through those lyrics, and that's what drove her performances, bringing forth those powerful deliveries of each song that moved the depths of our souls. And that's why some of Jenni's biggest hits weren't originals. For example, when she recorded "Ya lo sé," it had already been released as a banda song by another group, so Jenni turned it into a ranchera and she owned it. After a while, even mariachis thought it was a Jenni original, which only goes to show the extent of her powerful interpretations. She made each story come to life and sound like it was one of her own experiences.

Jen was an incredible communicator and performer, and she was primed and ready to take on bigger stages. It was time. She had already played the Ford Theater in L.A., but her dreams and aspirations went way beyond that stage: she wanted to reach the Gibson Theater, the place to play in L.A., but she wasn't quite there yet. I believed in her, and I needed Que Buena, the leading authority in Los Angeles radio for Mexican Regional music, to believe in her too and give her the support she deserved and needed to make her dreams a reality. I reached out to a friend who put me in touch with Eddie León, one of Que Buena's main programming directors. I had an in, so now I had to convince them to give Jenni a shot. Her brother Lupillo had recently criticized the station publicly over a business arrangement he had with them, but I was ready to prove to them that Jenni would be well worth their time and support. I knew she was on the cusp of becoming huge and was hoping they would get on board the Jenni train and help us see this through.

We finally got a meeting with the station directors, and I brought Jen because I wanted them to hear from her directly. Program director Pepe Garza, who became a big part of her life and career, had been hesitant to give her his full support, never imagining that the woman he knew as Lupillo Rivera's sister would turn the tables on everyone and jump to unthinkable heights of stardom. But he finally agreed to give her a shot, not before warning her, "Jenni, I can make you famous, but I can't *unfamous* you once my work is done. So what you do with that is really going to be up to you." If she managed it well, he said it could be a priceless investment in her career and life. She never forgot those words and he never forgot her. From that day forward, he became her mentor, one of the few people she'd turn to for honest feedback. She'd take her albums before they were released and play him every song, taking notes of his critique and suggestions. And he did so gladly, seeing that she was putting her heart and soul into her music and her career, quickly realizing that she was going to make it regardless of the obstacles she had to overcome to get there.

Great, Que Buena was finally fully supporting Jenni, but they knew she didn't have the draw to make it to the Gibson Theater just yet, so they suggested we aim for the Kodak Theater first. It was slightly more manageable with 3,500 seats and appropriate for where Jen was at in her career, while still being a prestigious venue. Being the ambitious woman that she was, Jenni wasn't too sure about this midway deal, but then they said the magic words: "You will be the first Mexican Regional artist to hold a concert there." Done. If Jen knew she was going to be the first at something, that was it, she was in, the deal was a go.

The Kodak Theater was a relatively new venue, the Oscars were held there, but it wasn't exactly Latino-friendly; however, Jen had faith that we would make it work. So we set the date, October 14, 2005. Regardless of how many times Jen had been knocked down, she was always filled with faith. She was a very spiritual woman and always had hope and faith accompanying her every step of the way. That meant all the way to her performances too. She never touched a stage without a prayer, and at every show, be it a bar or a stadium, she always took a moment of silence to visualize the stage and what she was about to do, kind of like a quarterback right before heading out to the field for a big game. She always had butterflies, she always was worried and wondered if they were going to like her, so this moment of prayer and visualization helped her focus and put her in the right frame of mind to go out and give it her all. And that's exactly what she did on that night at the Kodak Theater before hitting that stage and performing to a sold-out crowd.

Yeah, we did it, our first sold-out concert at the Kodak Theater! We were all on cloud nine. She had done smaller outdoor amphitheaters, but never anything like this. This was a full-on production with stage props and lighting, the whole nine yards, and she was involved in every single detail of the show: from the choreography, to how she would walk on and off stage, to the hard and soft lighting. And it worked. She owned that concert as if she had been playing those types of venues for years. She owned that stage. We were all so proud! It was like watching our young child graduate from kindergarten. From a management perspective, to have a venue like that in L.A. as a reference helped us book her at other places, and it kicked off the national tours. After seeing her handle that concert, I knew that we were well on our way.

Years later, I was talking to one of the Kodak Theater's head of security, and I was asking about some of the craziest moments they've experienced at the theater. Not knowing that I had been a part of it, he said, "One year, we had this Mexican lady and, man, all the audience members were women, and they all drunk, and we not only sold out the show but also all of the liquor. I've never seen so many women drink as much as that woman's fans!" I smiled because I knew exactly what he was referring to: Jen had not only been the first Mexican Regional act to perform at the Kodak Theater, to a sold-out crowd no less, but her concert also still holds the record for the most alcohol sold during a performance. That October 2005 night was such a fantastic milestone: it was the beginning of a career of sold-out concerts at prestigious venues and her launch to stardom. As if that night wasn't enough, that same month her album *Parrandera, rebelde y atrevida* debuted at number 20 in the Billboard Latin Album charts, grabbing the number 10 spot only a week later. Jen was on a roll with her music career, she was in love, and after all the heartache and hard times things were finally looking up. Maybe 2005 was God's way of giving her a break and letting her build the strength and happiness she would need to fall back on the following year, a year that would be filled with trials and tribulations. Who knows? All we knew back then was that we were at an all-time high and the time to conquer Mexico had finally arrived.

Chapter 5

La Gran Señora Conquers México

jennirivera
@jennirivera

Aun en Tijuana...intentando cruzar la frontera. Recordando el evento de anoche pienso: Que hermosa manera de celebrar su aniversario 123!! Mis respetos para los organizadores. El Sr Carlos Bustamante y funcionarios prepararon una fiesta en orden para su lindo Tijuana. Estoy honrada de que me hayan invitado! Dios los bendiga....siempre!! Los quiero!

2012-08-06

If making it in the United States had been difficult for Jenni, Mexico would prove to be an even steeper uphill battle, but she was ready to reach the top, and she wouldn't take no for an answer. Her sights were set on Mexico, her parents' homeland, a place rooted in traditions she had learned to know and love while growing up in Long Beach. And now she wanted to represent the perfectly imperfect woman in this macho world that demanded women to reach unrealistic standards of perfection. In the United States, she was slowly becoming the female ambassador of telling it like it is and keeping it real, and she was adamant about bringing her music and message to the ever elusive Mexican audience, one that was hard to win over as a Mexican-American artist from across the border, but Jen was willing, able, and ready to make this happen.

Gabriel Vázquez, her road manager, had connections in Mexico, so he started knocking on some doors to see what he could come up with; however, he was met with reluctance and skepticism. It was like starting from scratch all over again. Lupillo Rivera already had made a name for himself in Mexico, so Jen was once again only being seen as Lupillo's sister, regardless of all the headway she'd made in the United States. That counted for nothing in Mexico. Nevertheless, Gabo was persistent, and he was finally able to book a few dates in Nogales, Sonora, a city bordering Arizona where Jen's music had already managed to cross over, so they were eager to have her play there. That's when it hit Gabo—he could combine gigs in Arizona with this one in Nogales to make the most of this trip, and he could do the same with other towns along the border. That was their "in," that was how they would slowly make their way into Mexico, by literally crossing over and playing on both sides of the border.

The gigs in Mexico were small ones at first, which meant the budget didn't allow Jen to bring her own band, but Gabo was ready with a plan. He could book a local band to learn her music and play her gigs, but she'd have to arrive a day early to rehearse, which meant one less day at home. However, she knew that was the price she had to pay, so she was game. Her focus was on

Mexico, and nothing was going to stop Jen from befriending this audience, no matter how tough it got. Like the time she was set to play one of her first small gigs in Tijuana, and hardly anyone showed up.

Gabo had booked her at a venue called El Rodeo and had managed to have a local radio station sponsor the gig, but when the doors opened, the venue remained practically empty. Only a few loyal fans circled the room, but that was about it. Regardless, as was Jenni's style, she left her heart and soul on that stage, because even if there was only a handful of people, she wanted to show them how grateful she was for their loyalty and their presence, and she wanted to make sure they had a good time. Like in the United States, it was all about keeping her followers happy so they would help spread the word and bring more friends to her next appearance. Gabo felt embarrassed with the radio station for the poor turnout, but this only made Jen and him want to work harder; it was a challenge they were ready to take on, but in order to come out on top, they needed more fans to follow suit. At the end of the night, Gabo turned to Jenni and said, "You'll see, next time we come to Tijuana, it will be a very different story."

Gabo knew Jen needed more exposure in Mexico in order to garner more fans, so he decided to get her gigs at free events hosted by radio stations, called *macro eventos*, which featured big-name bands like La Arrolladora, Valentín Elizalde, El Recodo, and even Lupillo Rivera, who drew larger crowds, averaging ten to fifteen thousand people in one day. The lesser-known bands were booked as their opening acts; however, the later they got to play, the more exposure they would have. Gabo managed to get Jen into three of these *macro eventos*: Mexicali on a Friday, Ensenada on a Saturday, and Tijuana on a Sunday. Although these were all-day events, it got unbearably hot in those cities during the day, so most locals would wait till sundown to hit these outdoor concerts, also knowing that their favorite bands usually closed the shows. Gabo was familiar with how they thought, so he kept pushing to get Jenni one of these coveted nighttime slots. However, Antonio Zermeño Naranjo, aka El Pony, a local radio personality and also the man who produced these three events, was reluctant to give Jenni a better slot because he wasn't sure the audience would like to see a relatively unknown artist sandwiched between their favorite bands. He wanted to keep his people happy, but Gabo knew that Jen would be able to win them over. She just needed a chance.

Finally, that shot came on Sunday in no less than Tijuana. Jen had already played her set earlier that day, but Gabo had asked El Pony if they could stick around backstage just in case a slot opened up. He agreed, but said he couldn't promise anything. So that evening, as they checked out the other bands and waited around, El Pony approached Gabo and asked him, "Is she ready to go back on stage now?" Turns out one of the acts was running late, so suddenly there was a slot to fill, and it needed to be done in a hurry. Gabo said yes, quickly let Jen know, and in a blink of an eye, she was standing at the bottom of the steps, ready to take the stage. The announcer prepped the audience and asked for a big round of applause for ... "*La hermana de Lupillo, Jenni Rivera.*" Jen darted around and cast Gabo a steely eyed glance and then went on and did her thing. Gabo often says, "Had that look been a loaded gun, I wouldn't be here to tell the story." She couldn't believe she had to deal with that label all over again, Lupillo's sister, but rather than giving up, it only fueled the fire of her desire to make a name for herself in Mexico once and for all.

As expected, she owned that stage like nobody's business. With just the three or four songs she was allotted for this event, Jen not only managed to get her audience's attention, she was able to hold them captive throughout her set, ultimately winning them over because she mastered the art of communication. Regardless of how big or small the stage or audience was, she always managed to infect them with her authenticity, her magic touch. And El Pony, who was standing next to Gabo watching her in action, immediately picked up on this and said to Gabo, "You're going to have a great run with her, you'll see."

"Oh, I know," said Gabo. "One day she's going to make it real big. One day you'll see that all of these people will be here to see her and only her on stage."

Jen had such a great performance and was so ecstatic, that by the time she left the stage, she'd forgotten all about being announced as Lupillo's sister. Gabo recalls that day as if it were yesterday because of what an incredible job she had done, and also because it marked the beginning of her slow and steady rise in Mexico. However, there was still a lot of ground to cover to get this plane in the air.

In order to get more Mexican fans, Jen needed more local airplay, and in order to make this happen, we needed a healthy push from her record label, so we set up a meeting with José Behar, then president and CEO of Univision Music Group. As we sat in his huge corner office admiring the walls filled with plaques of artists who had been our inspiration for years, José walked in, greeted us, and started singing Jenni's praise for her rising career, but she cut him short and went straight to the point, as always, "José, I need to break into Mexico." He smiled and explained that it was a difficult market, different from the U.S. industry. So she replied, "If I don't break into Mexico, I'll have to become a stripper, and you don't want your artist to be a stripper, right?" There she went, flaunting that charm that made it so hard to say no to her. Like so many others, José caved. To this day, when I have a cafecito with José, he still says, "That woman just wouldn't take no for an answer. She would look at you with those child-like eyes, and it was just impossible to say no." So he promised to back her in Mexico and ask his team to start promoting her there, but that didn't mean it would be easy. For this whole move to be worthwhile, she would have to go on a promotional tour throughout Mexico, visiting each and every radio station, going on local TV shows, whatever needed to be done to help promote her work in person. José took a chance on Jenni, and we really needed his support and we got it. Now it was her turn to grab this opportunity and turn it into another success.

By then, we also had Arturo Rivera on our team, who replaced Yanalté Galván once their business relationship had run its course. Based in Mexico, Arturo was the guy in Mexican Regional music who had handled all of the big artists and had all the who's who connections and media influence to create Jenni's backstory and make sure she was known for her songs and her message, rather than for being Lupillo's sister. Breaking into this sexist market wouldn't be easy, and even less so as a woman trying to break into it through a machismo-laden music genre, but Jen had been dealing with the machismo deeply embedded in our Latino culture her whole life, so she knew how to be sexy and firm, and had the balls to handle it all like a pro.

Much like rock and roll, the competitiveness in banda music is palpable, and it was even harder for a woman. Everybody was looking at Jenni and thinking, "Yeah, okay, what are you gonna do, get naked to get attention?" And Jen was like, "No, watch me. Watch what I do." Jen didn't want any special privileges; she just wanted to be treated like one of the boys. She could drink like them and hold her own in their presence with her wit, charm, and straight-shooting ways, and she knew she could go head-to-head with them in this music genre too, because she had thick skin and a target audience none of them could compete with: women. Her songs, her story, her message was to and for women, an underserved audience who was ready to lap up all she had to offer because she wasn't just a celebrity, she was one of them. That ability to communicate with women on such a personal level had been crucial to her success in the United States and would also prove to be crucial in Mexico because with the women on her side, she'd also inevitably win over all the machista husbands, fathers, boyfriends, and that's exactly what happened.

Gabo and Jen set out on their first big promotional tour in Mexico, starting with Tijuana, Baja California, then moving on to Sonora, Sinaloa, Jalisco, Guadalajara, until they finally landed in Mexico City. And this was no joke, they were driving city to city and hitting each and every radio and TV station lined up on their promotional push. They needed to expose the media and public to Jen's wit and talent, and the only way to do so was to have her show up in person and charm their socks off.

Meanwhile, back at home, Jen was smack in the middle of her divorce with Juan Lopez and doing all she could to balance her work and family life and be as present as possible for her kids, so she decided to take her youngest child, Johnny, on this promo tour, to keep him close, comfort him, and spend some time with him. Johnny was only around three or four at the time, full of life and restless, like any other child that age, and there were no nannies or babysitters in sight, so it was a challenge for Gabo, to say the least. While Jenni did her promo interviews, Gabo would take on the role of babysitter, but sometimes Johnny would escape his watch and barge into the room interrupting the interview and sometimes even hogging their attention. He wasn't afraid of the mic or the spotlight, so much so that the hosts sometimes tried to interview him directly, but his Spanish wasn't good enough to carry a conversation, which didn't mean he didn't try. Gabo recalls that the only way Jen could manage to settle him down was by saying, "If you don't behave, I'm gonna have to go out and buy you a new dad." And he'd reply, "No, Mom, please, no!" That would quiet him down instantly because he adored his father.

Together, Gabo and Jen knocked on every radio station's door and promoted the hell out of her backstory and her music. They were working as a united front and they were unstoppable; it was them against the world in Mexico. Gabo babysat while Jen interviewed, then he went out and did public relations for her, and if the driver wasn't available for any leg of the tour, Gabo would hop in and drive them to their next destination, no complaints, no qualms, no reservations. They knew they had to roll up their sleeves and work hard, and that's exactly what they did. Their days started bright and early and ended very late, but they had to keep going.

As Gabo recalls, there were two songs they were pushing on this promo tour. The first one was "Qué me vas a dar si vuelvo," which was well liked, but at the time La Arrolladora was promoting their version of that same song. La Arrolladora was a well-known band in Mexico, so if the radio station had to choose between the two, since they couldn't promote both songs, many went with La Arrolladora. Even so, Jenni's version was becoming popular. Yes, it was a banda version of the song like Arrolladora, but the novelty was hearing a woman sing it. Nevertheless, La Arrolladora was stronger than Jenni, so Gabo decided their best bet was to push another one of her songs from the *Parrandera, rebelde y atrevida* album, "De contrabando," a Joan Sebastián song. Now that was the game changer we'd been looking for. "De contrabando" was a huge success and became her first strong hit in both the United States and Mexico. Jenni finally had secured a foothold in the Mexican market, and there was no stopping her now. The "Lupillo's sister" label was finally history, and the phone started ringing off the hook. We were not only being booked at bigger venues in the United States, but now Mexico wanted Jenni too.

With José Behar's support, Arturo Rivera's connections, and Gabriel Vázquez's direction in Mexico, Jen was being booked as the main act at county fairs and palenques, which are somewhat like rodeos and are all the rage in Mexico. This had never been done by a woman, and no one expected it would get the welcoming response it did. The Mexican audience usually veered from an older crowd who listened to ranchera music to a younger crowd who listened to pop, where sex sells, so when Jenni came along, she helped merge these two audiences with her sound, her charm, and her life story. As a mother of five, she was considered a *señora*, but she was also incredibly young at heart and knew how to communicate with the newer generations through her music. To top it off, she put on a show that was up to par with any other great Mexican performer; she had already accumulated a wealth of experience in the United States, so she had mastered her craft and knew how to handle her audience like a professional puppeteer, and they were smitten. Then, in Spring 2006, she got booked at a big palenque in Guadalajara, which was a smash success, and that's when we all knew she had done it. With the combination of her talent, charm, experience, and the right team, Mexico was now hers for the keeping.

Bigger and more frequent gigs meant more travel to and from Mexico, which also meant more days on the road with unexpected twists and turns. Gabo kept close tabs on Jen to make sure they made it on time to all of their commitments, but it was no easy feat, as Jen was always notoriously late, and he knew this. If they had to leave a hotel at 6:00 a.m. to catch a flight, Gabo would start calling her at 5:30 a.m. to make sure she was ready, and would then swing by her room only to find her frantically running around the room with her assistant tossing things into half-filled, open suitcases.

They'd eventually manage to dart out the door and, no matter how early they started their morning, they always arrived at the airport late, making it to the airplane just in the nick of time. Gabo would talk to someone at the airline counter or in the security line, explaining that they were late and if they didn't hurry, the plane would leave Jenni Rivera behind, and she wouldn't make it to her next show. Sometimes this worked, sometimes it didn't, but somehow, they always managed to make the flight. When they finally boarded the plane, Gabo recalls that Jen would use the flight time to either catch up on sleep or read. She loved reading self-help or spiritual books, anything that might inspire her and help her better her life.

Once they arrived at their destination, they'd check in to the
hotel and then, if she was hungry, Gabo always sought out a
restaurant that served the city's or town's classic dish. That's what
Jenni loved. So, if they were in Guadalajara, she'd want to eat
carne en su jugo; if they were in Monterrey, she'd ask for *cabrito
asado*. After chowing down, they'd return to the hotel, where
Jen would rest and then get ready for her show. Of course, they
would always have to rush out the door at the very last minute
to make it to the venue on time. When they were running late,
she'd prep in the car and hop out with her microphone in hand
and head in the game, walking straight to the stage to face the
antsy crowd. The audience would sometimes get rowdy and
upset at her tardiness, but would leave that all behind as soon as
they saw her on stage. That was part of Jenni's magic. She knew
how to win over her audience regardless of the circumstances.
They were enchanted by her charm and authenticity. Gabo often
remembers that sometimes, after spending a long time on stage
singing and drinking with her fans, she'd suddenly need to use
the bathroom, but instead of taking a calculated break, she'd
just straight up tell her concertgoers, "Hold on, I have to go pee,
I'll be right back," and she'd literally leave the stage, go to the
bathroom, and then climb back on as if it were the most normal
thing to do while performing, and the audience loved her for
that. They loved her for being that perfectly imperfect woman
they could relate to.

Once the show ended, if Jen was hungry, Gabo would make
sure to have something for her to eat, or they'd stop somewhere
to grab a bite, and then head back to the hotel, where Jen would
go straight to bed. As Gabo told me, "She would walk through her
hotel room's door, head straight to the bed, get under the covers,

and fall asleep instantly. She didn't even take the time to change into her pajamas. We could've all been in the room hanging out and chatting, and she'd have been sleeping placidly by our side." That was a typical day on tour with Jen and Gabo.

As I've mentioned before, life on the road, whether it was around the United States or Mexico, meant sacrificing time with her children, so she'd take every free moment she had to call home and check in on her kids. She made sure to always stay in touch with them, even if she was in another country. She constantly missed them. Yes, she wanted to follow her passion and do what she loved, but the price she had to pay, the sacrifice of not being with her children, pained her greatly, even though she knew that her success would provide them with a better life. For this same reason, even if she was doubled over with menstrual cramps or feeling under the weather, she knew that the show must go on. If she was going to sacrifice time with her children, you better be damn sure she was going to play every show and attend every event and meeting to justify her absence from home. Yes, she may have arrived late, but she always made it. Her work ethic was impeccable. She knew she was her family's provider, and they depended on her to put food on the table, and nothing was going to stop her, unless it was a medical emergency, something that Gabo experienced firsthand in Guadalajara in 2007.

It was Saturday and Gabo and Jenni were traveling from León, Guanajuato, to Guadalajara, where she was scheduled to perform on Sunday in a nearby town. When they arrived in Guadalajara, Jen had a really bad stomachache, but that didn't stop her. As usual, they checked into the hotel, then went to grab a bite to eat for lunch, and returned to the hotel to rest before they took off to the town where she'd be playing the next day. Gabo asked her if she needed anything, if she wanted him to call a doctor to check out her stomach issues, but she said no. She'd taken some pain relievers and hoped that they would kick in while she rested that afternoon. So they agreed to meet at 9:00 p.m. that night to continue their journey; however, two hours later Gabo got a call on his cell from Jen. When he answered, she said in despair, "Gabo, take me to the hospital, please, I can't stand the pain any longer, please take me to the hospital!" Gabo calmed her down, hung up, called some friends to find out what hospital would be best for her, then he called his assistant, picked her up, and drove straight to Hospital Jardines de Guadalupe. As soon as they walked into the emergency room, she was hospitalized. Given her symptoms, the medical staff believed her appendix had burst, and she had to go into surgery immediately; it was now a life or death situation. Gabo remembers that she was crying from the pain; it was unbearable. As they prepped her for surgery, she handed him her belongings, and in that instant her phone rang. Gabo picked up and it was Jacqie. He had to break the news to her.

"Your mom isn't feeling well. Her appendix seems to be the issue, and they're taking her into surgery now."

Jacqie heard him and then said, "May I speak to her?"

Jenni overheard Gabo's conversation and, through tears of pain, told him to give her the phone. Meanwhile, she was already on the gurney being wheeled toward the operating room. Jacqie had turned eighteen that day and was calling to tell her mom that now that she was of legal age, she had decided it was time for her to move out of the house. She wanted to be an independent woman and make a life for herself on her own.

"Princess, please, just wait till I get back home," Jenni pleaded as she was being rolled away.

"No, Mom, my things are already in the car and I'm about to leave now."

Jen couldn't believe her ears. She had no choice but to cut the conversation short because her surgery could not wait. As she handed Gabo the phone, she started wailing not only from the physical pain but also from the pain of not being able to be home to deal with her teenage daughter. Gabo did his best to calm her down until they took her into the operating room, and he had to wait outside.

That was the epitome of Jenni right there. No matter what she was going through, no matter how much pain she might be in, no matter how difficult the circumstances, no matter where she was in the world, she always tried to come through for her family. And this goes not only for her children but for her parents, siblings, and extended family too. If they called to ask her for money, she handed it over, no questions asked, even when the sums came to ten, twenty, or thirty thousand dollars. She felt it was her obligation to give back to them, especially when her star began to rise. And as for her children, although they never had to ask her for money, she always did her best to be there for them, no matter what, even if that meant taking a call from her rebellious teen as they wheeled her off into a life or death surgery. Her love for them had no bounds and no limits.

Fortunately, the surgery went well. Gabo had to cancel their Sunday show, Jen's mother traveled to Guadalajara to be by her side, and as soon as the doctor gave her the green light, they returned to Los Angeles.

Meanwhile, her popularity continued to rise. For her latest album, *Mi vida loca*, Rocío Sandoval "La Peligrosa," a Los Angeles radio host, had mentioned a song to Jen that had been a big

Chiquis, Gloria Solis, Jenni, and Jaylah.

Chiquis; Jenni's makeup artist, Jacob Yebale; and Jenni.

Edward James Olmos, Jenni, and Chris Perez.

Pete with the *Filly Brown* cast: Chrissie Fit, Lou Diamond Phillips, Jenni, and Gina Rodriguez.

Gabo and Jenni.

Gabo and Jenni.

I Love Jenni photo shoot: Jaylah, Jacqie, Mikey, Esteban, Jenicka, and Johnny.

Jacob Yebale adding his finishing touches to Jenni la Diva de la Banda before a performance.

Jenni and Pete, with her Premio Lo Nuestro 2008 award for Regional Music Female Artist of the Year.

Jenni's 40th birthday party. Clockwise from left: Elena Jiménez, Delia Hauser, Jacob Yebale, Pete, Gloria Solis, and Gabo.

Jenni after a sold-out concert at Nokia Live.

Jenni celebrating Jenicka's graduation.

Jenni being interviewed by Mario Lopez.

Jenni at her home office.

Jenni at the record label ready to get down to business.

One of Jenni's many donations to the Children's Hospital Los Angeles.

hit in Mexico and that she thought would be perfect for her. Jen listened to it, liked it, and decided to include it in this album, doing her own take of it in banda style. That song was "Mírame," and it also climbed the charts and hit number one in both the United States and Mexico. That was it, that was the beginning of the rest of her hit-making career. She kept them coming, her popularity continued to grow, and she was showered with a myriad of work opportunities; however, her personal life was in shambles.

Chapter 6

Trials and Tribulations

Jenni Rivera ✓
@jennirivera

"I'm infamous for falling...but I'm notorious for getting back up"....Jenni Rivera

10/7/12, 12:12 PM

241 RETWEETS **151** LIKES

↩ ⇄ ♥ •••

By Spring 2006, Jenni was well on her way to becoming a star in both the United States and Mexico. She'd played a sold-out show at the Kodak Theater, and had finally had her first big hit in Mexico with the song "De contrabando," opening new doors that allowed her to play an important *palenque* in Guadalajara, which was the start of many more tours and bigger stages in Mexico. As if that weren't enough, her album *Parrandera, rebelde y atrevida* had not only made Billboard's Top 20 Latin Album list, it had also gone gold in Mexico and gold and platinum in the United States. At last, her career was on course, and she was accomplishing her goals and making her dreams a reality. However, not as much could be said about her personal life.

In April 2006, her first ex-husband, José Trinidad "Trino" Marín, who had been on the run since she had filed a charge against him for sexually assaulting her sister and daughters, was finally caught and detained by the FBI. So, as her divorce from her second husband, Juan López, was finally settled on June 9, 2006, rather than being able to celebrate the closure of this chapter in her life and move on, the nightmarish court battle against Trino was slowly taking shape, a trial that began in April and would last fourteen months, quickly taking center stage in her life and the media.

Jenni Rivera's Ex-Husband
Found Guilty of Sexual Abuse

By the time this trial came around, I had already gotten to know Jenni better. She always spoke her mind, which made her genuine and endearing to fans, but also caused trouble when it came to handling her in the media. My instinct had always been to keep private issues as private as possible, so as to maintain whatever went public under careful control, but Jen had a different approach in mind. She had decided that she wanted to go public with this story with hopes of not only bringing justice to her family, but also helping other victims who had suffered the same criminal acts but were too afraid to come forward and let their voices be heard. Although sexual abuse unfortunately is not as rare as we would hope, it was definitely uncommon to speak about it openly in our Latino community, especially if you were a celebrity. But Jen was no average public figure. She didn't mind broaching taboo topics because she was a fighter, and she wanted to do what was in everyone's best interest, even if that meant she would be scrutinized by the media along the way.

It was a long and harrowing trial. They appeared in court once a month for fourteen months, and many in the media criticized Jenni for putting Rosie and Chiquis through such a public battle, saying it was just a publicity stunt to get more attention. Some even called them liars, but those allegations fell on deaf ears with Jen and she ploughed forward. I didn't agree with her method at first, but I wasn't working with her at the time, so I didn't have much of a say as her manager.

Jen and I had had a fallout earlier that year with respect to some award tickets. She was taking her family and also Gabriel, so I got upset seeing it as a favoritism play. However, I later found out Gabo had procured his own tickets. I probably should've let that go, but I pressed on, and we ended up butting heads. It wasn't serious enough to end our relationship, but it was clear we both needed a break, so Jen suggested I go work for her brother Lupillo for a while to see if I could help him reinvigorate his career, which had recently taken a turn for the worse. I accepted, appreciating the opportunity and seeing it as a challenge and a way to prove to her the value of my work. Nevertheless, Jen was my sister in every sense of the word—our bond was profound and strong—so even though we were mad and went our separate ways for a year, it was far from radio silence. We missed each other immensely and made it a point to remain in touch, showing up for each other when we needed support. Case in point, the Trino trial. I was there for her as much as possible throughout the trial, present on many of the court dates, by her side and ready to talk and help as needed. And, as always, I continued to give it to her straight and tell it like it is in hopes that my thoughts or suggestions might be of some help.

"Jen, I'm not so sure this is a safe subject right now. Your career is going so well, you don't know, this may all come at a big cost."

"It's something I have to do as a mother, Pete, not an artist!" she said, adamantly. "This isn't about my career. This is about a mother seeking justice for her daughters and sister."

I understood where she was coming from, I got it, but I was still hesitant because this didn't just involve her. Now her sister and daughters were going to have to face their mortifying past and abuser straight up in the public eye, forced to relive terrifying moments they had tried to bury deep within. So in their defense, I spoke up.

"But, this is about their lives, not yours, Jen."

"You know, Pete, if I don't talk about it, it feeds into the reason why our people and our community don't talk about it, and it's happened to so many others."

She understood they had agonizing days ahead of them, but she also refused to cower silently in the corner and let this asshole get away with it. The time had come to stand up to him once and for all, and also help others do the same in the process. That's when it clicked for me. I finally realized I had been reacting to the situation like all the other old-school and conservative members of our community, trying to keep this taboo topic quiet and in the privacy of their own lives, sweeping it under the rug, at a loss with how to deal with such an unthinkable situation. Out of sight, out of mind. But Jen was absolutely right. Someone needed to bring up the uncomfortable issues and face them head on, someone had to stand up and say that sexual abuse was not okay, it was not acceptable, and if it happened there were dire consequences to be faced, and that someone in this case was Jenni. She was breaking down walls.

"We have to talk about it publicly because that's how we're going to heal and make sure that other girls and victims in the future don't feel like it's their fault. I want everyone to know it's okay to speak up. No one should tolerate such abuse, ever," she said, tenaciously.

What followed was a hard-fought, dire, and emotionally draining ordeal. Jen was pushed to grow thicker skin and get as tough as nails. She couldn't afford to dwell on anything; she knew she had to press forward to find closure for her family and to get one step closer to forgiving herself for everything that had gone down. The abuse had started almost two decades earlier, and the time had come to put a lid on it and him once and for all.

Jen met and started dating Trino in 1984. She was fifteen and he was in his twenties, and the day she lost her virginity to him, she got pregnant. Just like that. Coming from a traditional family, she did what was expected of her and moved out and in with him, got married, and took on the responsibility of wife and mother, while still trying to graduate from high school, even though he kept insisting her new role was to stay home and forget about school altogether. Then, she began to suffer domestic violence. He'd slap her around, beat her, until one day in the summer of 1992 she finally had the courage to leave him for good. By then, she already had three children with him. However, this wasn't the end of their drama. Five years later, she found out that he had not only been beating her, but also sexually abusing her sister Rosie and her daughters, Chiquis and Jacqie. Jen was absolutely devastated. Little did she know this was to be the cross she would bear for the rest of her life, never forgiving herself for not being able to prevent and protect her sister and daughters from such trauma.

That's what made this trial so important to Jenni. Not only did she want closure for all of them, she also wanted to speak up publicly and try to help give other victims the courage or voice to get the help they deserved. I firmly believe that this is one of the reasons Jen became such a strong voice for Latinas. It wasn't just about her music. It was her stance and the action she took to voice their problems and concerns and fight discrimination, abuse, and the countless other injustices these women were quietly suffering. That's exactly why she had older Latina women who were Dominican or Cuban or Puerto Rican who couldn't care less about banda music but were huge Jenni Rivera fans. Even though they never heard her sing, they'd heard her story on Don Fransciso or Cristina's shows, and they could relate, together with the single mothers and those suffering abuse or betrayal. She represented them and hence became the voice for a multitude of women spanning different generations and countries. When she brought this trial to them via the media, her message was clear: it was time to stop grinning and bearing it all; it was time to speak up and break that old-school silence that was eating them up inside; it was time to seek justice.

So, while she was touring the United States, conquering the Mexican stage, and rising to the top of the charts for the first time in her career, she scheduled all work-related meeting and events around the court dates. Whether she was traveling to Mexico or performing locally, she made sure to stop her activities just in time to attend each and every one of those dates for the following fourteen months, always with her family by her side, supporting each other every step of the way. I was there on many of these days, seeing it all unfold firsthand, and I remember finding it extremely difficult to watch Rosie, Chiquis, and Jacqie relive those painful traumas of their past. Many nights after those court dates, Jen would vent and express her concerns with me in one of our heart-to-heart talks. She was especially worried about Chiquis, who seemed to be the most affected by all of this. Jen wanted to comfort her, but found it to be extremely difficult. It was hard for Chiquis to come to terms with the fact that the man who should've been her healthy father figure, the one who was supposed to protect her from all harm, was the culprit of her unbearable trauma.

By May 2007, the jury came back and gave Jenni the gift she was hoping to receive that Mother's Day: Trino was found guilty of 6 of 9 counts of sexual assault and rape. And by June he was sentenced to thirty-one years in prison. I was in the room when the verdict was read and will never forget Trino's reaction. His stone-cold face revealed absolutely no emotion or remorse. Nothing. It was incredibly chilling. Meanwhile, on the Riveras side of the court, their eyes welled up with relief, and Jenni finally broke down and let the tears stream freely down her cheeks. She had spent the last fourteen months as her family's pillar of strength, absorbing all the blows and criticisms, steadfast and with her eye on the end goal: putting this monster in jail. Nothing would make this mother hen back down, she had charged ahead at full force, and was now finally receiving the closure she and her girls deserved.

The trial most definitely brought a concrete end to this hellish period in their lives, but its aftermath had long-lasting effects on all of them. Jacqie kept asking why he'd done such a thing. She was too young to remember the abuse she suffered, but she still wanted to make sense of it all. Meanwhile, Chiquis yearned to be able to forgive him. She hoped to have the chance to visit him one day, have an open and honest talk, and finally say to his face, "I forgive you." However, she also felt conflicted, even more so with her father's reaction, as well as how his family handled the entire situation. They never stopped calling her and Jen and Rosie liars, accusing them of making all of it up to screw Trino over. It was debilitating to the soul, to say the least.

However, there was also an unexpected silver lining after the trial: more victims gathered the courage to come forward. It started with other Marín family members speaking out against Trino and how they too had suffered through his abuse. And then came an outpouring of letters from people who, after seeing the trial in the media, had felt compelled to share their stories of abuse and rape, some even begging for help. It was painful, eye-opening, and somehow comforting to finally have it all out in the open and realize that they were not alone.

Love Can't Conquer All

Meanwhile, life continued to unfold, and as Jen dealt with this tormenting sequence of events in 2006, she managed to accomplish yet another dream: she was finally booked to play the Gibson Theater on August 5, 2006, and performed to a sold-out crowd. Despite having worked tirelessly to achieve this dream, she was still incredulous that so many people continued to turn up to see this girl from Long Beach do her thing on stage. She was absolutely over the moon with joy. But success was always somehow bittersweet for Jen. Aside from the ongoing, gut-wrenching trial, Jen's love life was also coming undone.

Jen and Fernando had been in an "on again off again" relationship for the past three years. It was tumultuous at times, but their love for each other always seemed to win the day, until the summer of 2006. That was the first time they left each other for such a long time, taking a six-month breather to figure out what they wanted and how to best approach their situations. The timing couldn't have been worse for Jen. She would've loved to have her soul mate by her side to celebrate her triumphs and support her through her tribulations. At long last, as 2006 came to a close, Jen caved and reached out to Ferni for support, in hopes of getting back together, never imagining she'd find such a changed man in his place.

Fernando is a great guy, but back then he was challenged by the battle of addiction. Jenni knew this and stood by him, always offering to take care of him, but he had pride. In all the time they were together, Ferni never depended on Jenni and he wasn't about to start now. He always tried to figure out a way; however, when it comes to heavy drugs, sometimes you just can't go at it alone.

We all have demons that we want to outrun when we should be facing them, and I think Fernando's drug addiction was basically an escape from his insecurities and a way of decompressing from the stresses of life. When Jen met him he was already smoking weed, and as the years passed, his addictions got worse, moving on to heavier drugs, which started messing with his personality and their relationship. Nevertheless, even if they were on one of their infamous breaks, Jen was always there for him, always a phone call away. If his mom called asking her for help, she would jump in her car and go pick him up and bring him home or take him to rehab. She never sent anyone; she did it herself. And she'd go to the projects where they lived and check up on him in the following days to make sure he was doing okay.

However, when she reached out to him at the end of 2006 and they tried to give their relationship another shot, Jen quickly realized that his latest addiction now involved crystal meth. Talk about a whole other ball game, totally out of Jen's or anyone's league. He'd wake up in the middle of the night screaming, paranoid, thinking that she wanted to kill him, hallucinating and saying that he knew she had called her brothers and asked them to kill him. Jen would tenderly and patiently calm him down and explain that he was having a night terror and that everything was okay, that no one was trying to kill him, and that he should try to get some rest. Seeing him like this was heartbreaking for Jen. All she ever wanted was someone to take care of her and make her feel safe, and she had honestly thought that Fernando would be that person. She was tired of being the one who took care of her men, the one they depended on; it was a role she no longer wanted to play in her relationships. This was one of the reasons her relationship with Fernando had become so volatile. Deep down she knew that his addictions hindered him, and that wasn't the type of man she wanted her kids to grow up with as a role model. He had so many amazing qualities, ones that made her feel whole and happy and understood, but this issue was too big to ignore.

Imagine finally finding your soul mate only to discover you won't be able to be with him? A telenovela has nothing on this story. Fernando was the love of Jen's life, the man of her dreams in so many ways, her musical muse, her best friend, but she finally came to terms with the fact that she had to call it quits with him for good. The crystal meth addiction was uncontrollable. He needed professional help, but it wouldn't work unless he made that decision for himself, and staying by his side and coddling him would only be a detriment to his recovery. So, by early 2007, Jen made one of the hardest decisions of her life: she left Fernando for good. No more back and forth, no more on again and off again, it was done. She did this to protect herself, to protect her children, and, ultimately, to protect him. If his loved ones hadn't had the strength to back off and let him hit rock bottom, he probably wouldn't be around today.

Ending their romantic relationship was heart-wrenching, but their bond was too strong to cut all ties completely, so they managed to remain friends. If Fernando was in trouble, Jen was the one bailing him out of jail. She put him in rehab numerous times; she put all her resources at his disposal in hopes that he would get better. He was a good guy with a good heart and Jen knew it. That's why, even though she had to give up on their love, she refused to give up on him.

So, as 2007 unfolded, Jen not only had to break it off with her soul mate, she had to sit back and watch him unravel before her eyes until he ultimately decided to take matters into his own hands and seek professional help. Meanwhile, Trino was found guilty and sentenced to thirty-one years in jail, which brought some relief to her inner turmoil; however, just when the dust seemed to be settling, her ex-husband Juan Lopez was caught drug trafficking and in October 2007 was sentenced to ten years in prison. Yet somehow, throughout this roller coaster ride that drove Jenni to the top in her professional life only to bring her racing down on a personal level, she continued to hold her head high and charge forward. She was the definition of resilience, and I know she couldn't have done it without her faith; her children, who were her reason for living; and her work. As life continued to hit her with one-two punches, she managed to bob and weave, and come back stronger, making a name for herself, rising to the top, and letting her entrepreneurial spirit soar.

Chapter 7

Bossing It Up! A Business Magnate in the Making

jennirivera
@jennirivera

"I've never done anything worth doing by "accident"...nor did any of my accomplishments happen by accident...they occured through hard work".....;-)

2012-08-15

N o matter what Jen had going on in her personal life, her entrepreneurial spirit never slept. When things got hard on a personal level, her work became her safe haven, a place where she felt she had everything under control, with a group of people she knew she could rely on. Here she could breathe, forget about what was troubling her at the time, and focus on her passion: making shit happen. From the start of her life, Jen saw her parents tirelessly working and was inspired by her dad's steadfast work ethic and entrepreneurial spirit. When she hit her early teens, she started hustling with her father and brothers, selling cassettes and CDs at the local swap meet and hawking event-specific merchandise when the opportunity presented itself, such as the 1984 Olympics or during the Menudo craze, where she made buttons and sold them to her junior high classmates. Little did she know all this training would serve a purpose later in her career.

As the years went by, her hard-knock life made the hustler in Jen thrive, and when she finally decided to give her music career a real shot, she channeled all this energy and experience into her newfound path, eventually mastering the art of selling herself as a brand. She started small and worked her way up, from concert merchandising and her own cosmetics line to reality TV and her own radio show. There was no stopping Jen; she poured herself into her work, constantly creating, coming up with new business ideas, eager to see them through, a real business magnate in the making.

Every successful person has a backstory that fuels their goals and ambitions. Her number one incentive was her children, but the real fire that kept her burning the midnight oil was the fear of falling below the poverty line again. The dread of reliving that day-to-day uncertainty, wondering if the welfare check will be enough to pay the rent and put food on the table, kept Jenni going till the day she passed away. She never wanted to subject any of her children to those dire circumstances again. Those living conditions were a thing of the past, and she worked hard to make sure they stayed there.

Jen's drive was so forceful that I couldn't even keep up with her at times, and I consider myself a full-on workaholic. This woman really never stopped, so much so that eventually the word *exhaustion* in my vocabulary was replaced with *aguantar*, to endure, because that was the only way I could stay on track with Jen's pace. I'm talking about a woman who woke up at the crack of dawn and went to bed past midnight, taking care of her family and working nonstop with only a four- to six-hour break at night for some shut-eye.

A typical day in the life of Jen when she wasn't on tour started at 5:00 a.m. She kicked it off with some devotional time reading passages from the Bible, then squeezed in her workout, and later headed over to the kitchen to make breakfast for her kids. By 7:00 a.m. on the dot, without missing a beat, I would get a message from her, ready to start the workday full speed ahead. I always thought that she partly wanted to make sure I was awake and ready to go, 'cause once she got started there was no stopping her. That first message or BBM—back then we both had Blackberrys—varied from either a simple "Good morning" to an outline of what we had in store for the day. The only reason I didn't receive this morning greeting was if she was on tour and in flight, because she would even text me from Mexico—and weekends weren't an exception either.

By the time regular work hours were underway, Jen had already taken her kids to school and answered all her e-mails. As the day progressed, if I wasn't by her side, we would touch base at least ten times a day, while she followed up on pending issues, made phone calls, headed over to interviews, meetings, whatever needed to be done to continue developing and promoting her career. And yeah, she was known for being late, but she always made it. She could've used the single mother card and countless other excuses to cancel meetings or interviews or events, but she had her priorities straight. These were her obligations, it was what helped her put food on the table, so backing out was out of the question. That's what made her a hustler before anything else.

She dove in so deep that there was never a clear end to her workday, sometimes not even making it home till 11:00 p.m., but that didn't stop her from keeping up with her motherly duties too. Jen would check up on her children throughout the day, and relished every second she spent with them, be it in the morning when she made breakfast for them and drove them to school, or in the evening when she shared some precious time with them before saying good night. Now, just because she tucked them in didn't mean that she'd call it a day for herself too. Her nights had no set routine. It wasn't like she would put her phone aside and stop working. Sometimes she'd shoot out messages to me at one, two, or three in the morning. Her mind just never seemed to shut down. As she lay in bed, staring at the ceiling, urging herself to disconnect and fall asleep, that's when her creativity would reach its peak. I would get the most random texts in the middle of the night with an idea she didn't want to forget, or something she wanted my feedback on, or a reminder of what we needed to get done the following day. When her eyes finally felt somewhat heavy, she'd place her phone on her nightstand and sleep, only to be up and at 'em all over again the following morning at 5:00 a.m. sharp.

That was Jen, a workhorse with a creative and entrepreneurial mind that was constantly thinking up new projects and business ventures. It was unbelievable. She was always doodling in her old-school planner, writing notes about her life, jotting down ideas, drawing jeans and dresses for her future apparel line, always in production mode, not only creating but also trying to figure out how to bring these ideas to life. It was such a part of her essence that she didn't know how to turn it off. Even on vacation, she'd continuously drum up new ventures, never disconnecting completely or taking a real break from it all. At times this became a liability because she would run herself into the ground with this nonstop approach to life and work, but she felt the need to be hands on with everything she set out to accomplish.

Jen understood from early on that in order to emulate the success stories she so admired, such as Jennifer Lopez's career, she had to keep her eye on the ball. She may not have been the one negotiating the deals—that was usually my role— but everything that was on the table had been reviewed or requested by Jenni herself. If her signature was needed, you best believe she knew what was going down. Nothing happened without her final okay. She diligently did her homework on the particular business she was starting up, so she could walk into subsequent meetings well informed and ready to hit the ground running.

Jen's goal was to expand her brand past music and offer her Mexican Regional fans merchandise and products that had long been available for the general U.S. market, but not for them. In this way, she was set to be the first to make such a move in this music genre. She kept her finger on the pop-culture pulse and closely observed the Kardashians' entrepreneurial success and how artists such as Beyoncé ventured out of music and into various other business endeavors, and she knew she had what it took to follow those footsteps. Let's not forget, before becoming an artist, she was a college-educated businesswoman. She understood how commerce worked and had the know-how and natural business savvy to put her ideas in motion, and that's exactly what she did.

When I first came on board, she had already launched her first business venture, her concert merchandise line. As a child she had seen her father grab a Polaroid camera at the end of his workday and head out to the nightclubs to take photos of the patrons in exchange for some dollars. This memory stuck with her, and when she launched her music career, she applied it to herself in hopes of making some extra cash at each of her gigs, and it worked. She'd meet her growing number of fans after every performance, take a Polaroid picture with them, and offer it up as a memento for twenty bucks. It became so successful that some promoters and security teams at certain venues began to ban this photo op because they didn't have the resources to handle the growing crowd, but that didn't stop Jen. She'd just turn to her fans and say, "Meet me at the gas station down the block," or she'd ask them to find her at the nearest taco truck, and they did. Hundreds of fans would line up for a chance to take a photo with their idol, and she stood there and smiled for every last one of them, making their dream of meeting and interacting with her come true while generating five to seven thousand dollars of extra revenue a night. After taking note of the Polaroid photo-op's popularity, she decided to develop her own concert merchandise, giving birth to her first business venture outside of singing and recording.

As she became more successful in her music career and began to develop new lines of business, one thing was clear: Jen never solely envisioned these ventures to pad her pockets. They usually surfaced from ideas that would ultimately support, cater to, or provide an opportunity for others in her community. Of course she benefitted from all she did, but if she could figure out a way to provide jobs or give back to her community, her fans, her friends, her family, she didn't think twice about it. Such was the case with her first cosmetics line and real estate venture.

When Jen came up with Divina Cosmetics, she didn't just want to sell products to her people. She wanted to give them the opportunity to be empowered by these products and be a part of this business venture. She envisioned a line that followed a multilevel marketing plan, such as the Avon or Mary Kay business model. When she was a kid, Jen had seen her mom sell Avon products on the side to generate extra income for their family; she knew what a difference this could make in a struggling family's livelihood, and she wanted to extend this possibility to others who were suffering similar circumstances. Unfortunately, the managers she selected weren't successful, so she ultimately had to shut down operations and put Divina Cosmetics to rest, but her vision and heart were in the right place.

Then, another interesting opportunity presented itself. One of Jen's close high school friends, who worked in real estate, approached her asking her for her support to get a broker firm off the ground and running. In this case, Jen didn't have to invest capital, she just had to lend her celebrity status to the venture in exchange for a royalty fee. Jen not only saw this as a good, low-risk business opportunity for her, she also knew it could be a great service for her fellow Latinos. She had worked in real estate, she knew the market, and she knew all too well how intimidating it was for Latinos to step into a bank and ask for a home loan. Lending her image and brand to a company that would help make the lending and buying process Latino-friendly was a no-brainer in her eyes, and that's how Divina Realty was born. The intentions were good, the deal was solid, but no one was able to foresee the big housing market crash of 2008. When Jen realized that some of the loans handled at this company were questionable, she decided to withdraw herself from this agreement and stop promoting this firm, but she let them keep the name.

Meanwhile, with Jen's finger always on the pulse of pop and urban culture, a new idea sprung to life: it was time to try her hand at perfumes. Artists like Beyoncé and Britney Spears were coming out with their own fragrance lines, and Jen wanted in. She put together a plan and put her daughter, Chiquis, to work. Chiquis was instrumental in developing Jen's fragrance line. While Jen continued her tours, performances, recordings, and media blitzes, Chiquis took off to China to carry out the necessary research and gather the information they needed to make this dream a reality. She put in a lot of hours and eventually helped Jen launch a perfume line that to this day is still on the market and available for purchase, becoming one of Jen's first successful and long-lasting business ventures.

Another one of her successful business endeavors, which is still alive and thriving, is the Jenni Rivera Tequila, but we sure hit quite a few roadblocks before being able to get that one off the ground! One of Jen's staple moves during her concerts was downing shots of tequila with her audience. They loved her for that, and she loved creating such an intimate setting for them, no matter how large the venue. Once her career took off and her fan base was off the charts, it only seemed natural for us to seek a tequila endorsement deal for her, but we never thought it would become such an uphill battle. I reached out to all of the brand ambassadors, but no one was biting. Why would they pass up such a lucrative opportunity? It didn't make sense. She played sold-out shows where concertgoers downed tequilas like water— let's not forget the record-breaking alcohol consumption at the Kodak Theater!—but the company executives just didn't get it.

HER NAME WAS DOLORES

Ever the creative genius, Jen decided to entice them further. She recorded a song called "Chuper Amigos," where she mentioned practically every tequila brand in the lyrics, then we put some images together with her and the brands and went back out to market possible partnerships … to no avail. We all knew Jenni's pull and how easily she would up the sales of any brand that would deem to endorse her, but none of them dared to take the plunge. Frustrated at their lack of vision, as I further analyzed the situation, I realized that most of these companies were controlled by general market agencies or agencies located on the East Coast, and neither knew Jenni Rivera was such a household name in the West Coast and Mexico. They hadn't heard of her yet, so they weren't willing to take such a risk on someone who they believed had yet to achieve the celebrity status of the likes of Shakira.

We also suddenly noticed another underlying problem: machismo. Yeah, while the tequila brands were saying no, no, no, counteroffers from several wine labels started pouring in. It was clear that these execs thought it more appropriate and feminine for Jen to go with a wine label than tequila, but they didn't know Jen. Sure, she'd have a glass of wine here and there with a meal, but she wasn't really a wine drinker. Her go-to drink was hard liquor, especially on stage. It represented her music, her performance, her message to her fans, so she wasn't about to sell out and sign off on a wine endorsement. She chose to remain true to herself and simply wait it out, which paid off in the end.

Veronica Nava, one of Jen's good friends, managed to secure an endorsement deal for her with Nuvo Vodka. True, it wasn't tequila, Jen's first love in the hard liquor world, but at least we kept it in the family, so she went with it. The initial deal required

119

Jen to feature the vodka in one of her music videos; however, when we realized how this move had affected Nuvo Vodka's sales, we agreed to extend the agreement to include endorsing the brand at her shows for a full year. The company did so well it was sold to Diageo spirits, the world's largest producer of spirits, for millions of dollars, yet Jen didn't see a dime because she hadn't negotiated to receive a percentage of the sale. You live, you learn. That's when Jen decided to take matters into her own hands, cut out the middle man, and create her own brand of tequila, approving the label design, the tequila, all of it. Jenni Rivera Tequila was in the works when she passed away. It hit the shelves after her accident and is still available to this day. Another successful business move, another great vision, another step closer to becoming a renowned business magnate.

After these first ventures, licensing opportunities finally came a knocking. Up until this point, Jen had equity in everything because she wanted to be able to control the products that carried her name, but it was time to open up to other business opportunities. The established brand BH Cosmetics expressed interest in working with Jen and proved to be a good partner and smart choice for her. Had she not left our world so soon, this profitable venture featuring her line of cosmetics and hair appliances would've likely had a longer run.

Meanwhile, parallel to these endeavors was Jen's dream of providing a line of clothing that would help dress her fans to the nines, and that's how her apparel line was born. Her ultimate goal was for Latina women to finally feel good about themselves, to at long last learn how to embrace their God-given curves and feel sexy inside and out. I don't think I ever learned so much about body types than as in those initial meetings when Jen started planning her line of jeans, from the muffin top and the pear to the apples and the bananas. Who knew fruit could so perfectly describe them all? One thing was clear from the get-go: Jen didn't want her fellow Latinas to feel the need to change their bodies; she simply yearned to see them feel comfortable in their own skin.

What was great about this venture is that Jen got it. She understood the struggle on a personal level, often going on tiring escapades in search of a simple, well-fitted pair of jeans. She'd observed and celebrated Jennifer Lopez's Kohl's clothing line launch, hoping this might be the solution she and her fellow Latinas so desperately needed, but was quickly disappointed. The pieces looked expensive, but the quality was poor, and Jen was a stickler for quality. She had a hunch this line wouldn't last because of this main issue, and she was right. That's when she decided to take matters into her own hands.

Jen built from experience, she was very meticulous, and she made a point to learn from other people's mistakes. So she hired a fashion designer and set out to create a high-quality and flattering line of jeans for her fellow Latinas, jeans that would celebrate their curves and make them look and feel stunning. She was as hands-on in this venture as any other or more, participating in the selection of material, tags, zippers, buttons, and keeping a close eye on the quality control of the jeans themselves, trying to make sure the end product faithfully reflected her vision. It was very near and dear to her heart, but unfortunately she passed away without seeing the line's official launch, which happened after her accident, together with another big dream of hers: opening her own boutique. This last plan was in full motion before she passed away. It was to be a place where she would sell not only her jeans, but also other apparel, such as tracksuits—her go-to style while on the road and at home—and dresses, as well as her fragrances and eventually her own shoe line. The sky was the limit.

The Jenni Rivera Boutique was set to open in Panorama City, a predominantly Latino community, perfect for her merchandise, and only a fifteen-minute drive from her house. As with every business, she was hands-on with this one too, together with Chiquis's tireless efforts and support. When she passed away, prior to the boutique's opening, I honestly found it all to be a bit eerie. I couldn't help compare this to Selena's story, the Mexican-American singer who had been murdered shortly after opening her own boutique. This was yet another one of Jen's great ideas that she never got to see flourish, but her family followed through for her, and the Jenni Rivera Boutique is still open to this day.

The Diva's Blossoming Media Empire

Jen had already ventured into perfumes, cosmetics, and had her tequila, apparel line, and boutique in the works. Now it was time to build her media empire, expanding her charm and magic into television, radio, film, books, and more!

I Love Jenni

The first time we considered venturing into the TV world was when Latin World Entertainment, the same company that manages Sofía Vergara, approached us about doing a reality show. The proposal piqued Jen's curiosity, so we went along with the idea, attending meetings to pitch this idea to different cable networks; however, the executives didn't quite know what to do with our angle. They weren't sure how a Latina mother of five with Jen's history would translate to TV, so, although they had expressed initial interest, everyone we reached out to politely declined. Discouraged by the rejection, Jen opted to shelve the TV world for the time being and continue focusing on her many other ventures.

Nevertheless, a few months later, I gave the idea another shot, approaching it from an angle we hadn't previously considered: executive producers. It was less of a risk for Jen. If the show tanked, as executive producer it was less likely that her name would be splashed all over the media, and she found comfort in this option. She didn't want to expose her career to a major hit or miss, but was definitely interested in exploring this new outlet, so she asked me what I had in mind. "What if we cast Chiquis and her friends to represent Latinas in L.A.?" Jenni hesitated at first. Always the protective Mama Bear, she asked me to first run the concept by Chiquis herself to see how she reacted, and then we'd go from there. Chiquis wasn't too convinced, saying she was comfortable working behind the scenes at home, but I insisted she give it a shot. I knew she had something special. She just needed to be coaxed out of her shell. Chiquis was kind of shy, somewhat of a girl-next-door type, so I introduced her to my friend RaqC, a radio host back then in L.A. She was a red-head Salvadorian with a firecracker personality who would complement Chiquis well and had radio experience, which meant she was good on air and knew how to interact with others and hold her own, so it was settled.

Once every party agreed, I went to my friends at Mun2, Telemundo's bilingual channel, and pitched the show. I expressed my concept and added that Chiquis and one of her friends would carry the show, and Jen would lend her name as an executive producer. They liked what they heard and gave us the green light to shoot a pilot, which showed well, so we moved on to the next step: filming the first season of *Chiquis and RaqC*. We were all set and ready to roll, and things were moving along smoothly, when RaqC began clashing with production. We did our best to navigate the tension, but it got so bad that we ultimately had to let her go midseason, which left us with a whopping hole to fill in the remaining episodes. That's when Jen came to the rescue. She just stepped in to pick up the slack, but her presence on the show became so crucial to its success that it eventually organically morphed into *I Love Jenni*, the first reality show featuring a Latina and her family, another milestone for Jen's career, another one she hit out of the ballpark.

As *I Love Jenni* took off, Lieberman Broadcasting, which also owned the radio station Que Buena, approached Jenni in 2011 with the idea of hosting her own talk show for its channel Estrella Network. That was music to her ears! She was keen on the idea of becoming the Mexican Oprah Winfrey, and this seemed like the perfect platform to get the ball rolling. They said she could bring in her own producer and they'd build a special set for the show. The pay wasn't great, but the opportunity was hard to pass up, so she was all in. However, as soon as production began, Jen quickly realized she didn't have the creative control she'd been promised, and it all went south from there. Jen simply refused to continue working on something that wasn't true to her heart, so she called it quits. We had a discussion with the company's owners and the show's producers, which ended in a standoff and ultimately a lawsuit against Jen for breaking the contract she had signed by refusing to tape more episodes. However, after many tense exchanges, we finally agreed to settle with them. She no longer had to continue the talk show, but she had to agree to be a judge on *Tengo talento*, one of the network's talent shows. Done deal. She recorded thirteen *Tengo talento* episodes, fulfilled her obligations, and moved on to greener pastures. Meanwhile, her budding goal to become the Mexican Oprah Winfrey found a new home: radio.

Contacto Directo con Jenni Rivera

By the time *Contacto Directo con Jenni Rivera* hit the airwaves, Jen became a media queen by all accounts: sound recording artist, television, and now radio. Previous offers to do radio had fallen through until Gabo and one of Jen's good friends, Nestor "Pato," suggested we reach out to Entravision Communications. Good things come to those who wait, and now it was Jen's turn. They struck a deal and her radio show was born.

Like always, she was hands-on with everything, from choosing the topics to bringing her sister Rosie in as a cohost as well as her long-time friend Diablito as one of the producers. It worked like a charm because there was a familiarity on air among them that made it relatable, authentic, and plain old fun. Jen's show aired once a week and covered a range of topics, including fashion, relationships, pop culture, and more. She loved it. The show was her way of staying in touch with her fans, supporting her colleagues in the music industry, and playing the music she enjoyed. Furthermore, it was the first time a woman had a nationally syndicated show with more than a million dollars of advertising in the first year—that's just unheard of in the industry—another huge milestone in Jen's thriving career, another media platform under her wing. Little did she imagine that the movie industry would come a knocking next.

Filly Brown

Acting had never really crossed Jen's mind before. She had a slew of ideas and business ventures in the works, and definitely had some experience in front of the camera with her reality show, but she never thought acting was in the cards for her, until she received a call from none other than Edward James Olmos. Edward had signed up to work on a project titled *Filly Brown*. It was a small independent film with relatively unknown actors, with the exception of himself and Lou Diamond Philips. As the director and producers were putting together the cast, Lisa Ríos, one of the movie's executive producers and a friend of Jen's from the world of radio, threw Jenni's name into the basket for the role of María Tenorio—that's when Edward perked up and quickly chimed in. He knew who she was and also remembered that his daughter went to school with Jen's kids in Encino, so he offered to reach out to her.

Never in her life had Jen imagined that renowned actor Edward James Olmos even knew she existed, so when she got his call she was floored and flattered. As they spoke, he mentioned the film and asked if she'd be interested in being part of the cast. "I think you'd be great for the part." Jen had no acting experience, so she was hesitant, but he assured her, "Don't worry, I'll make sure you're okay. I'll make sure you get whatever coaching and classes you need." Stunned, Jen kept thinking, *Is this true, is this really happening? Is Edward James Olmos personally inviting me to participate in this film and offering to be my guide as I venture into my first movie role?* It was an offer she simply couldn't refuse, so she finally decided to jump right in with a resounding, "Yes!"

Ever the good student, Jen enrolled in some private acting classes and, to her astonishment, discovered that she was a natural. Huge relief, but the real hurdle was still before her. She was cast to play María Tenorio, Majo Tenorio's mother, an abusive and manipulative woman who takes advantage of her responsible and loving daughter. As Jen started reading the script, doubts began to cast shadows in her mind; she wasn't sure if she'd be able to pull this off successfully. This woman was a criminal and an absentee mother who took advantage of her daughter, while Jen lived and breathed for her kids. It had nothing to do with who she was in real life, so she struggled to figure out where to draw her inspiration. When we talked about it, I said, "Jen, you just gotta be everything that you're not." And that's exactly what she did.

Jen stepped into those two days of filming prepped by her classes and pumped by the challenge, and she absolutely nailed it! Suddenly, another door had opened in Jen's career, one that involved acting–a role we would have seen develop further had she made it to 2013. On December 4, 2012, a few days before Jen's fatal accident, we announced a big deal with ABC proclaiming Jen as the first Latina lead in her own sitcom. Another first, another milestone, another goal cut short by her death.

Other projects that were also stunted by Jen's passing included her stint as a judge on the second season of *La voz... México*; her dream of having her own record label, where she could serve as producer and mentor to new and emerging talented artists; and her goal to finally finish and publish her memoir.

Unbreakable

Jen had started writing her autobiography a few years prior to her death, randomly, on scraps of paper, in her planner, jotting her thoughts down when inspiration hit, whether she was on a plane, tour bus, commuting, or in a hotel room. She'd send me e-mails and text messages with her musings, things she didn't want to forget, and I'd make sure to save these snippets for her, acting like a hard drive for her memories.

After some time, I noticed she had a lot of material, so I sat her down and said, "Jen, we're ready. Let's get this book thing done." I introduced her to Jeff Silberman, who is now my agent, and they immediately hit it off. We knew Jen had an amazing story, one that would grip anyone's heart, regardless of whether they were a Jenni Rivera fan or not. Fortunately, Jeff recognized this potential, so he moved forward and set up meetings with publishers for the three of us to pitch the book with our contagious enthusiasm … but once again, we were met by yet another bunch of top executives who just didn't get it. They were reluctant to take a chance on her, doubting how well it might do in the market, unable to see Jenni's power and draw and the millions of fans who would have eagerly purchased her memoir. And they remained blind to her magic … until she passed away. As soon as the media outlets exploded in a frenzy covering her accident and the countless fans sharing their devastation and adoration for la Gran Diva, the phone started ringing off the hook. Suddenly every publisher in town wanted a piece of the action, ready to pay premium prices to release her story to the world ASAP.

I had the manuscript, the collection of notes and thoughts that, once weaved together, would narrate Jenni's amazing story, but I no longer had a say on what should be done with it because, after Jen's passing, it belonged to the estate, which was handled by her sister Rosie. All I was asked to do was pass along everything I had and make the necessary introductions. Rosie and the Rivera family took over from there.

It's no secret that I have my reservations with regard to what they finally published as Jenni Rivera's official autobiography, *Unbreakable: My Story, My Way*. It was her story, but it wasn't her way. There were many missing pieces, many untold stories, many key people in her life who were barely, if at all, mentioned. It's clear to me the family had a heavy hand in the editing stages of this book because I remember her original ideas; they're fresh in my mind, and they didn't feature her siblings as prominently as in the official published version because they hadn't been there in real life either. Her family and work life were two different worlds. The family didn't really participate in her career development, with the exception of Chiquis who was her rock, because Jen didn't burden them with all the struggles she had to traverse to make it big. That's what her work family was for. She protected, provided, and cared for her family, and when the cards were stacked against her, she leaned on her work family for support, but her book painted a somewhat different picture.

That's why I'm here, sharing her story, the one that I saw with my own eyes, the one that shows how passionate she was about her children and her work. Jen was a force to be reckoned with, she waged a difficult battle to make it big, and when she finally clinched her hard-earned success, she quickly realized nothing was ever or would ever be a win-win situation in her life. Soon enough, she would have to come to terms with the fact that becoming a business magnate and star also carried its own set of sacrifices and pitfalls.

Chapter 8

Success Comes at a Price

Jenni Rivera ✓
@jennirivera

"I'm a woman all the time...I'm a
Diva sometime's....and I'm a bitch
when you ask for it."....#jenniFACT

8/15/12, 2:10 AM

304 RETWEETS **180** LIKES

↩   ⇄   ♥   •••

Many people believe that once you've made it, you're all set, your worries are gone, and your life is all smiles, but in many cases, major accomplishments come with sacrifices, and big success stories come at a price. The biggest price Jen had to pay was being away from her children. That was the one that caused her the deepest pain. That was what she fretted about the most each time she had to go on tour and leave them behind. But that wasn't the only price she paid. No matter where you come from, when you become successful, many people around you suddenly feel entitled to a piece of the action, be it family, friends, colleagues, fans ... or Mexican cartels.

It's hard to strike a balance between feeling indebted to those who helped you when you were down and the needs and nature of your business. In our Latino community, most of us have been raised to believe that if someone gives us a hand—especially from the beginning, either when you first arrived to the United States, when you're down on your luck, or when you're setting off to pursue a dream that requires a lot of work and sacrifice—we are eternally indebted to them for their support. And Jen wasn't the exception to this unspoken rule. She couldn't turn her back on those who had helped her along her difficult path to success. Her loyalty was her trademark, and that remained true even after she made it big.

I tried to talk some business sense into her, explaining that those debts and that sense of gratitude eventually get paid off; they don't have to be a lifelong thing because that can get tricky real fast. After a while, some people may see these gestures of indebted gratitude as something they are now entitled to; they begin to expect handouts and help no matter how much or how little they did to help you when you were down on your luck. There are certain characters in our lives who may have simply given us one meal when we really needed it, yet make it a point to continuously remind us of that meal and that generous gesture, so long as they can continue cashing in the favor for the rest of their days. They're like leeches. We all know at least one person like this, feeding off of other people's success. However, Jen sometimes seemed naïve when it came to seeing people's true colors. I wanted to make sure she was aware of people's intentions. I didn't want her generosity to be taken advantage of, but I also completely got where she was coming from.

In our Latino community we are instilled with a sense of loyalty since birth. We learn to use a specific bank because that's the one our parents went to when we were young, unlike second- or third-generation Americans who shop around for the best deal for their circumstances. No, we're taught to stay loyal to one institution because it treated our family well, and that means more than any other better deal we may be offered. I came to realize this nature in our culture when I went to business school, and I learned that it was okay to switch banks or go to another market. However, I also discovered that our culture is inevitably embedded in our business practices, making the line between what's best for us and our blind loyalty quite a blurry one.

As savvy as Jen was in business, those cultural gaps were hard for her to comprehend from an entrepreneurial standpoint because no matter how far she came, she was adamant about never forgetting her roots and her humble beginnings and helping those who were there for her in the past. I have to be honest, I wasn't always for this way of doing business. I told her it was okay to be a little selfish. Sometimes, when you're constantly trying to solve other people's problems, you don't realize that you may actually be hindering their progress. They come to depend on you and only you to save them, when in reality what they need is to learn how to save themselves. But that was Jen, she was all heart, even in business, and as much as this burdened her at times, it was also part of her magic.

As her manager, however, it was a catch-22 situation. I wanted her to wake up and smell the coffee, but I also didn't want to change her essence, that approachable side that everyone knew and loved. You could find her at a 7-Eleven or at a taco truck any day of the week because she never forgot where she came from.

Her hood kept her grounded. Yet I couldn't ignore the slew of people who sponged off of her success, and that bothered the hell out of me, but there wasn't much I could do because it mostly stemmed from her family.

When Lupillo's success was on the rise, the family established a unique way of supporting each other: fifty percent of whatever he earned as a musician went to his pocket, and the other fifty percent went to the family pot. So when he made it in the industry—the first one of the Riveras to finally make this music dream a reality—he also became the biggest family contributor and, therefore, their ultimate breadwinner and god. As Jenni used to say, "The family was all on Lupillo's nuts." She observed from afar as she continued working hard on her own to make a name for herself, and once she did, the tables suddenly shifted.

As Jen climbed the stairs to stardom, she was not only providing for her children, but was also now becoming the biggest contributor to the family pot. Move over Lupillo, there's a new goddess and breadwinner in town. Now, whenever they were in a rut or needed cash for any other reason, they would all turn to Jen. And I'm not talking about just her immediate family. I'm talking about aunts, uncles, nieces, nephews, even friends and employees. They'd all come running to her with requests in the thousands of dollars, five thousand here, ten thousand over there. I couldn't believe their audacity, but Tía Jenni always came through for them. In all the years I worked with Jen, I saw her say no very few times, especially if the person was family. She could never turn her back on them, even when it was obvious they were crossing the line and asking for way too much. Her heart was made of gold, and she never made a move without considering how it would affect those around her, including her employees.

Once she became a star, Jen had thirty-three employees working for her, including her band, drivers in Mexico, office employees in California, and more, and she took her role as their employer very seriously. Jen knew that those paychecks they received helped provide for their families, so she couldn't slip up. If she didn't make money, they didn't make money, and if they didn't get paid, they couldn't put food on their tables for their families. She saw this ripple effect so clearly that, in addition to all the responsibilities toward her family, she carried the weight of being a provider for her employees too. She strived to make enough bank to keep food on her table as well as on theirs; she wouldn't have it any other way. She was amazing. And yes, in many ways Jen was Wonder Woman, but what many forgot along the way was that she was also human, and there were moments where the weight of feeling responsible for so many lives was too much for her to handle.

One time when she broke down in front of me, completely burned out, I turned to her and said, "Jen, you need to stop. Look, this is what you need to understand. If you can't do it anymore and you need to take a break, then take a break. Everyone else will figure it out, myself included." But she wouldn't have it. She wouldn't allow herself to take a break. She couldn't do that to her employees and even less so to her family. She couldn't let them down, and there was no way in hell she would dare do anything to risk losing it all and falling back into that dark hole she'd worked so tirelessly to dig herself out of. Being broke again was absolutely inconceivable in her mind. The bitter taste of those past days was always present in her life, pushing her to keep going. Even after becoming a multimillionaire, she still worked as hard as if she were living on her last twenty bucks. So taking a break was out of the question, no matter how much her body and mind were crying out for some much needed rest.

Now, wait a minute. I need to make one thing clear. Jen was kind and generous, but she was far from a pushover. Sure, she would always help her family and those in need by giving them money or jobs to make sure they were okay, but if you crossed that line with Jen, if you pushed her far enough to her limit, as much as she hated that type of confrontation, she'd let you go in the blink of an eye. Such was the case with one of her first publicists, Yanalté Galván, when she decided to jump ship and work with Graciela Beltrán. At first she was trying to juggle them both as clients, something that did not sit well with Jen, given her history and rivalry with Graciela and also her goal of having a team that worked exclusively for her. But she gave Yanalté a pass, knowing that she needed the work, and Jen couldn't afford to take her on full-time just yet. Eventually, the conflicts of interest were too deep and Jen finally said, "*Ya basta*, it's over."

Here's the clincher, here's where Jen's heart of gold comes into play. Regardless of all that went down between them, she still let Yanalté keep an SUV that technically belonged to Jen. Yanalté was like family to her, and she wasn't about to take away the one vehicle she needed to transport her special needs child. So, yes, there had been a heated exchange and she ultimately fired her, but she continued making payments for Yanalté's SUV for around one or two years. That was the Jen I knew.

Now let me backtrack a minute. In order to understand the weight of this issue, and why it was such a disappointment to Jen, we must dive into one of Jen's most public feuds, and one of our biggest media wrangles yet.

Jenni Rivera vs. Graciela Beltrán

Graciela Beltrán was originally one of the recording artists who had signed with Cintas Acuario, Jen's father's record label. He was awestruck with Graciela, always gloating about his *niña*, giving her music his full attention and backing her every move. Jen observed this from a distance and found it hard to accept and digest this relationship, especially when she herself was trying to break into the music industry with so little family support. But rather than vying for her father's attention, Jen remained focused and persevered like the little engine that could. When Jen decided to take her singing career seriously and become a full-time recording artist and performer, instead of letting Jen be, Graciela began to poke the dragon.

Suddenly, if Jen and Graciela were scheduled to play the same event, we'd get word that she didn't want Jen anywhere near the backstage area until she was done with her performance. I am a witness of how she continually dissed Jen, giving her dirty looks, not wanting to cross paths with her at events, and it was totally unnecessary. Jen was just starting out, while Graciela was already a full-fledged artist on the scene. She had a name, she was at the height of her career, there was no need for this type of treatment, but it was clearly a power trip, and she reveled in it. That's exactly why when Yanalté decided to take on Graciela as a client, Jen was none too pleased.

However, with time and hard work, the balance of powers began to shift. As Graciela's fame declined, Jen's star power was on the rise, and it was in that crossroads that they had their major face-off. Graciela, the media's little darling, was suddenly losing ground to Jen, the scandalous outspoken diva, and she wasn't having it. So she played the victim card, trying to garner as much attention as possible to keep her career alive. However, as Graciela used her girl-next-door image in the media in her favor, she also continued to antagonize Jen. It was like walking by a fence with a chained dog on the other side, purposefully kicking the fence to instigate the dog when no one is looking, then acting surprised and scared when the dog begins to growl and bark.

Jen allowed Graciela to get under her skin, and played right into her rivalry ploy, feeding the media frenzy when her growl turned into a roar with her song "Los ovarios." In that song, Jen refers to Graciela, who was known as "La Reina del Pueblo" (The Town's Queen), by saying "*Y las que se dicen ser reinas / son de un pueblo abandonado*," which basically translates to, "and those who call themselves queens / come from an abandoned town." The song is basically stating that those who dare mess with her don't know the size of her ovaries. In it, she laughs off all the trash talk and tags her rivals as insignificant now that her fame is soaring. Gabo and I cringed when we heard the song. We knew Jen was better than this, but, in classic Jenni style, rather than thinking it through, she reacted and pounced like a lion on her prey.

"Why do you want to stir up more trouble?" Gabo asked Jen after the song was released.

"I'm just doing what the rappers do. They have it out in their songs," explained Jen.

"Yeah, that's accepted in American culture, but our Mexican culture takes offense at this type of sassiness. They see it as a lack of respect. I know you're gonna do whatever you feel like doing at the end of the day, but just know I don't agree with this move," said Gabo.

As we expected, Graciela jumped at the chance to get the media to side with her after the song hit the airwaves, appearing on TV shows wailing against Jen's cruel and uncalled-for lyrics. Rather than letting her cry it out and leaving it alone, Jen jumped in to defend herself, explaining she'd had enough with the way Graciela had disrespected her for so long, but it ended up playing against her. The media began to question Jen's actions, wondering why she did this, why she needed to go there now that she was famous and Graciela's career wasn't what it used to be. Even some of her fans started turning against her for acting so arrogantly. Simultaneously, Gabo and I continued trying to talk some sense into Jen. Graciela's career was going nowhere, and Jen's actions were only helping Graciela remain relevant in the media. Gabo and I knew that as soon as she stopped feeding this feud, Graciela would go away, and the media's focus would move on to the next big headline. It was time for Jen to lay this to rest and take the high road, and she finally got it. Since then, Jen took on a neutral role and never allowed Graciela back into the game. And that was that.

The problem with Jen was that she was always quick to react, too quick for her own good. If she was hit, she'd hit back harder and go straight for the jugular. This happened with friends, lovers, family, employees, and, as much as she loved and appreciated them, her fans were no exception either. If they were out of line, she was the first to call them out, but she didn't think before she acted, and that sometimes got her into gratuitous trouble.

Jenni Strikes a Fan with Her Mic

It happened in Raleigh, North Carolina, in June 2008, at one of Jen's concerts. She was happily performing to her crowd of adoring fans when suddenly someone flung a beer can onto the stage and hit one of Jen's band members. Jen took matters into her own hands, but this time she went too far, and the media had a field day.

Truth be told, Jen had a history of dealing with her rowdy fans in her own way. Stuff like this happened often, since early on in her career. I remember one gig she had in Las Vegas where a macho guy threw a cup of beer at her and, without blinking an eye, she dropped the mic and darted straight at him. I dropped everything and ran behind her, trying to catch up, thinking, *What the hell just happened?* When it came to the fight or flight reaction, Jen always chose to fight; she never took anything sitting down, never took shit from anyone, even less so from her fans.

Gabo recalls another incident where a fan threw a lemon at her. She stopped the concert, brought the fan on stage, and slapped her across the face, right then and there, only to find out later that the lemon had a message written on it, "Jenni, I love you! Could you sing my song?" The fans were excited to see their idol and some were quite drunk, so they would do anything to call her attention, not thinking about the consequences. That one fan didn't throw a lemon at Jen aggressively, but how the hell are you supposed to interpret that when you're on stage and a flying object suddenly strikes your leg? Another time, a fan threw an ice cube at her and her reaction? She poured a glass filled with ice over his head. I kept telling her, "There are people who are hired to handle these situations. You can't interfere. You've gotta let them do their job. Even if they do something wrong, it's on them. It's not your responsibility, because if you intervene, then you become liable and people can sue you." But she also wanted to be heard. She would be damned if she felt someone was taunting her. She grew up with boys, she was a tomboy, she knew how to defend herself, and she wasn't one to back down from a fight or confrontation. If Jen felt threatened or attacked, she didn't take it quietly. She fought back because she wanted to teach her reckless fans a lesson. Everyone was usually buzzed at her concerts, and they usually laughed these confrontations off, until the North Carolina incident where things unintentionally took a turn for the worse.

I wasn't there that night, but Gabo was, and he remembers how it unfolded as if it were yesterday. When that can flew on stage and hit one of Jen's band members, Jen stopped the song in its tracks, faced the audience, and said, "Let's see if the person who had the balls to throw this can on stage has the balls to raise his hand and come clean." Now, Jen's audience was used to her joking around with them, and many jumped at the chance of getting close to her, exchanging a few words, or being invited on stage, so when she said this, four or five people raised their hands. Jen turned to one guy and asked, "Was it you, *m'ijo*? Was it you?" And he said yes. "Bring him to me, please," replied Jen. He thought it was all in good fun, as did the rest of the audience. They didn't think it was serious, but no one messed with her or her band members without suffering the consequences.

As soon as he climbed on stage, Gabo recalls Jen saying to him, "*M'ijo*, tell me something. Do you like it when someone bothers you while you're working?" "No," answered the guy. "*Pos*, neither do I," she said, and smacked him on the forehead with her mic. The guy managed to react before being hit and turned his head to avoid the mic, but wasn't quick enough, so it landed on his eyebrow, and blood immediately started to trickle down his face. He was quickly removed from the stage by security, but when one of the guards noticed he continued to bleed profusely, he called 911. The ambulance arrived together with the police, who asked who had done this to him. Gabo remembers that most people remained quiet, except for one of the security guards who came forward and said it had been the artist.

When Jen left the stage that night, she was met by these two police officers who questioned her and immediately arrested her for assaulting a fan, regardless of who had started it. As soon as they drove her away, Gabo grabbed the venue's promoter and Jenni's brother, Juan, and they followed the cop car to bail her out. Meanwhile, inside the precinct, as the officers took her mugshot, she made light of the situation, posing for the picture and asking if it was a good take. After a few hours, once they finally released her, she walked out and said to Gabo, "What's up? What happened? Let's go grab something to eat," as if it weren't that big of a deal, not even thinking about the possible consequences of what had just gone down.

As the dust of this incident began to settle, I suddenly got wind that the guy was lawyering up and preparing to file a lawsuit against Jen. I reached out to Jen to give her the bad news, and was surprised by her incredulousness.

"He's the one who threw the can. How can he sue me?"

"Yeah, but you're the one who hit him on stage with a mic, and you're the famous one that people see as a payday, Jen."

She argued with me at first, but I told her she needed to think about it with a clear head. "Everything you worked for that you did for your kids, well, this is now going to cost your kids. Your actions are going to cost your kids."

The whole situation really frustrated me. She was already famous, and there was no need to behave this way. How could she not see it? But she finally did. After all our back and forth, plus the threat of a lawsuit that would now affect her own kids, she realized she had to do something to take care of this once and for all. At last, she admitted that her actions were wrong and personally called the guy to invite him and his family to attend her next concert at Nokia Theater in L.A. It was actually an all-expenses paid weekend, which included a day at Disneyland. The guy accepted and they let bygones be bygones. Little did Jen know that yet another media scandal was already brewing and would soon hit her like a ton of bricks. The price of fame.

The Sex Tape Scandal

It all began with a phone call Gabo received from a promotor and friend in Mexico: "Gabriel, there's a video going around of your artist, and it has some pretty heavy stuff on it. Musicians have been circulating it on their phones."

"Wait, what are you talking about?" said Gabo, completely taken aback by the call.

"*Pos*, it's a porn video of your artist, *güey*."

Stunned, Gabo asked if he was sure it was Jenni, and his friend said yes, so Gabo asked him to send it over. His friend was hesitant at first; he didn't want people thinking he was the one who had started all this, but he finally texted and e-mailed it to Gabo. Meanwhile, Gabo had to figure out a way to break the news to Jen. At first she asked if he was sure. When Gabo explained that he'd asked for a copy to confirm the rumor, she simply said, "Check it out and let me know what's up."

Jen was not only like a sister to me, she was like a sister to Gabo, so having to watch this video made him feel extremely awkward, but Jen insisted. She needed to know if they were bluffing or if there really was a video. So Gabo obliged, and once he received the video, he hesitantly pressed play. In the first scene, she had her clothes on, and her friend was filming her while she spoke on the phone. It was definitely Jen. Then, after she hung up, things started getting a bit more hot and heavy, and that's when Gabo stopped the video and called Jen and said, "You had a white T-shirt and red pants."

Suddenly it all came back to her in a flash. It was a video she had filmed with a guy she was seeing at the time, one of her band members. He was a younger, good-looking man who had caught Jen's attention. She had simply been having a good time with him. He made her feel sexy and daring, so she was just going with the flow, forgetting that she was already Jenni Rivera the celebrity and just enjoying this newfound adventure. She didn't think twice about the consequences if this tape was ever leaked to the press. She was just living in the moment. To top it off, the fling came to a screeching end when Jen found out that the guy had lied to her about being separated. Gabo was the one who broke it to her. "Jen, this guy is married." At first she thought that Gabo was being as protective as always, so she didn't believe him, but he insisted, until she finally understood that the guy had been lying to her all along. She broke it off then and there, never thinking it would all come back to haunt her later.

Turns out the guy had a hidden agenda all along. She was just a pawn in his game. His goal was to get with the boss, Jenni Rivera, to better his position in life. Who knows, maybe at first he was hoping to build a solid enough relationship with her to become her go-to guy and reap those benefits, but that dream was cut short when she found out he was still married. Nevertheless, he still managed to make out with a humiliating video, and now he was ready to cash in.

When the sex tape surfaced, we also found out this guy was trying to sell it to the media. He'd offered it to Univision for around nine thousand dollars, but the deal fell through because we stepped in and intervened, releasing a statement explaining that the video was taken from a phone that was stolen from Jenni. Since the phone was personal property, if anyone published this material, they'd be implicated in the lawsuit. No one in the media touched it. Meanwhile, we also received a call asking for five thousand dollars in exchange for the video, but we already had it, so that bribe was quickly squashed. We were suddenly putting out fires left and right. Ultimately, the video did make the rounds online, but at least it didn't hit the media outlets.

Meanwhile, Jen was mortified at first. She couldn't believe she'd been so naïve about this guy. She never imagined he could be capable of such a thing. But what shamed her the most was having to tell her family about this whole scandal before the news hit the press. She called a family meeting and explained everything, breaking down into tears and asking for their forgiveness. But no one in her family or team judged her. We were all there to support her. She knew she had screwed up, and now it was time to move on. She never allowed it to shame her again and eventually even managed to crack jokes about it, saying it was a tutorial on how to keep your man satisfied. That was Jen right there, a perfect example of how she always managed to gather herself after a fall, get right back up and keep going. As she once wisely said, "If you're gonna give me lemons, I'm gonna make me some lemonade, with a shot of tequila."

Cartels and Jen's Run-In with the Law

There's a reason the catchphrase "Mo' money, mo' problems" exists. As Jen's career thrived, she not only felt responsible as a provider for her entire family and employees, she not only had to deal with bigger media headlines like the feud with Graciela and the altercation with her fan on stage, she not only had to handle people coming out of the woodworks trying to make a buck from her celebrity status with a sex tape, she had even bigger fish to fry: she had to learn how to handle with care the growing number of important people attending her concerts, which in Mexico meant drug lords and their families and lovers.

When Jen's popularity took off in Mexico, the army of women drawn to her message and concerts included none other than daughters, girlfriends, wives, and lovers of renowned Mexican cartel bosses. They became fans and regulars at her shows, and now they wanted to meet her. Gabo recalls these first brushes with the cartel families as polite yet edgy and intense. They'd send their people backstage to talk to Gabo, and he'd arrange for the family to meet Jen after the show, and she always obliged these requests. As outspoken and forthright as she was, Jen knew that it was best not to mess with these guys and their families. The families ranged from two to a dozen people, but no matter how many of them showed up at her dressing room, Jen always stopped what she was doing and posed for a photo or set aside a little time to chat with them. Keeping them happy kept all of us safe and, in turn, they were always respectful.

Then came the invitations to play at private events, birthdays, quinceañeras, you name it. Gabo managed these invites and found ways to politely decline some of them, explaining that Jen's schedule was completely booked, but there were some that we did accept. It was hard not to. Jen was first and foremost a savvy businesswoman, and it was difficult to turn down gigs that paid so well. It was a lot of damn money. However, these private parties were no joke. First off, we decided that Gabo would be the one to go with her, as he has a smaller build than me and has less of an intimidating presence than my own six-foot, three-hundred-pound self. We didn't want to ruffle any feathers. The idea was to get Jen in and out of there as quickly as possible. Some bands were basically held captive at these parties, entertaining the bosses until their lips and fingers were swollen from hours of nonstop playing, not daring to say that they were done for the night for fear they might lose their lives. But this wasn't the case with Jen for two main reasons: she was a woman and they knew she was famous. This meant a busy schedule, it meant she had other shows to get to the following day, so they were happy with her coming in, knocking it out of the park, and then heading home. And they were always very respectful, never demanding songs, but rather making requests. She also had her secret weapon: Gabo. He knew how to handle these situations and events, using his wit and charm to his advantage to secure and get out of any potentially harmful situations. He was a strategist, and I trusted him because he knew what he had to do, and he got it done.

The thing about Mexico is that it's truly littered with cartels. They are unavoidable. Aside from private parties, there were also times she had to deal with police raids in her own concerts. One time, during a palenque performance, Jen was up on stage doing her thing when all of a sudden we noticed this man dashing up the stairs followed by men in full military garb bounding after him. As he weaved through the crowd, people parted to let him by and then closed the way to slow down the Federales who were hot on his trail. It was like watching a live action sequence. And all the while, Jen didn't skip a beat. She kept belting out her song while giving us sideway glances trying to figure out what the hell was going on. But the show must go on, and the way Jen handled the situation actually helped the concertgoers remain calm instead of entering into mass panic. Once the concert was over, we heard that the Federales had gotten word that El Chango, a wanted cartel member, was attending her concert. I wish I could say this was the only time this happened, but it wasn't. Since she became popular with the cartels, several of her shows suffered police raids and made the news. That's why the media oftentimes tried to link Jen to the cartels, but she wasn't in cahoots with them. They were simply her fans.

The media always made such a big deal about this possible link between Jen and the cartels that after her death, there was even speculation that renowned cartel leader, Edgar Valdez Villareal, aka La Barbie, had been involved in her accident. This theory was based on a previous rumor that he had allegedly assaulted her at a concert, but neither were true. It was just the media trying to create headlines that didn't exist. I can't emphasize this enough—the cartel leaders and members were just Jen's fans. Every one of the people in these organized crime networks that we dealt with throughout the years were nothing but respectful toward her because she was a señora, a golden rule in the cartel world: you don't mess with señoras, you respect them. So she was never considered a threat to them. She never celebrated one cartel over another. She was just a woman talking shit about men in her songs, and they got it. They all had women in their lives who were Jenni fans because she was the only woman out there who was ballsy enough to speak her mind, and they all loved her for that.

Nevertheless, this was a heavy world we were dealing in, and it also came with a few scary moments that hit too close to home. Between the cartels and the corrupt government, it was often hard to tell who was who and what was what, which made it difficult to calculate if certain threats Jen had to face were real or fake. Like the time Mexican immigration officers detained her at the Mexico City airport claiming she had forgotten to declare the fifty thousand dollars she was carrying with her. Man, the media sure had another field day with that incident. What they didn't know was that Jen did declare that money, but they stopped her anyway. They knew who she was, so they thought they could scare her into handing over some of her cash. They basically asked her to pay a *multa* in order to get by them. Yeah, they were straight up asking her for a bribe in exchange for her safe passing and threatened to detain her if she didn't pay up, thinking that she would rather fork over some bills than let the media get wind of such a story, but they sure as hell didn't know Jenni. She looked them straight in the eye and said, "I'll stay here as long as it takes, but I'm not giving you a dime."

So they seized her money, took her into custody, and the media spun the story to attract more readers, but the truth was she had done nothing wrong. We had proof of payment from each performance contract, and she hadn't broken any laws. She just outright refused to give dirty cops money that she had rightfully earned and declared. Not one to give up, Jen hunkered down at the station, ordered pizzas for everyone, hired a lawyer, and simply waited it all out. That's why in the media shots you can see her smiling and waving because it was just another ploy to extort money from her, and she would be damned if she would take part in that. They eventually let her go and two weeks later had no choice but to release her seized money without getting away with a penny of it. She called them on their bluff and came out victorious; however, making these types of calls weren't always that easy. Sometimes we weren't sure who to believe or trust and had to go with our gut, making spur of the moment life or death decisions and praying for the best possible outcome.

Death Threat and the DEA

I will never forget that day in July 2011. We were prepping everything for Jen's upcoming trip to Mexico, another sold-out palenque show in Reynosa, Tamaulipas. I was going about my business, checking e-mails and voicemails when I heard our booking agent Michael Scafuto, with his old-school New York Italian accent, say: "Pete, call me back as soon as you get this. It's urgent." I returned his call immediately and noticed that he sounded scared. "Dude, the DEA contacted my office. They're looking for Jen. They said they need to get a hold of her ASAP about a very serious matter." He gave me the DEA's number, we hung up, and I instantly dialed Jen.

"What's up?" she said.

"I got a call from Michael Scafuto. He was contacted by the DEA, and they said they need to speak to you."

"Come over," she said.

I hung up, got in my car, and drove over to her house. We walked to her office, closed the door, and I made the call. I asked to speak to the special agent who'd left the message and explained what had happened, but he insisted on speaking to Jen directly. I was hoping to act as a buffer, hoping Jen wouldn't overreact with whatever news they had for her, but I obliged and gave her the phone. They exchanged greetings and he cut right to the chase, explaining that they had received a credible lead from a confidential source that there was a planned hit on her at her performance in Reynosa that weekend. She literally froze as she continued listening attentively. The agent advised her not to go. He emphasized once again that this came from a very reliable source and clarified that if she decided to ignore this warning and go regardless, they wouldn't be able to protect her once she crossed over to Mexico because they had no jurisdiction there. It was their responsibility to let her know about this credible threat, but it ultimately came down to her decision. Jen gracefully thanked him, hung up, and panic set in.

Not only did the agent repeatedly say that they had received this news from one of their credible informants on the ground, we also knew that this was the same palenque where singer Valentín Elizalde had been gunned down in an ambush shortly after his performance in 2006. This venue already had a dangerous reputation, even less reason to take the DEA's warning lightly. As we gathered ourselves after the initial shock, Jen called her lawyer in Mexico, Mario Macías, filled him in on what was going on, and asked him to check his sources to verify if the rumor was indeed true. Apparently, the local promoter swore up and down that they knew nothing of such a rumor and assured Mario that nothing would happen, that Jenni would be safe in their plaza.

By now, we had no idea who to trust, especially with Jen's life on the line. We kept going back and forth on possible decisions, scenarios, and outcomes. If she canceled out of the blue, the local promoter would know something was up, and the last thing you want is for those in Mexico to suspect you may be working with the feds, especially in this line of business, where you're out on stage and completely exposed to any and all dangers and threats. So that was out of the question. Then we thought we could maybe cancel and blame it on the weather. A huge storm was pounding Mexico that week, causing airports to shut down left and right, so we figured mother nature might be able to help us get out of this mess.

After thinking long and hard, we decided to go with this last option. Jen called the promoter directly, carefully explaining that she'd heard the Reynosa airport had been shut down due to the storm, which was true, so her private jet wouldn't be allowed to land safely. She apologized for this huge inconvenience and offered to return their deposit for having to cancel the show on such short notice. We thought we had it in the bag, until the promoter replied, "Don't worry, we've already made arrangements to open the airport and allow your plane to land." Jen was speechless. No way in hell we'd thought of this possibility. Just knowing that the promoter had pulled strings to authorize her jet to land, regardless of the inclement weather and airport shutdown, gave us the chills. Was the DEA right? Why were they going out of their way to get Jen to Reynosa? Was her life really in danger? She thanked the promoter for the special arrangements and hung up. Now what?

Not only was the show still a go, but her band had already been bussed in from another Mexican city, so if this threat was

152

real, they were already smack in the middle of harm's way. Jen was loyal to the core, never one to leave anyone hanging, so she decided to bite the bullet, take a leap of faith, and go. However, as brave as she appeared, Jen was also terrified. She asked Mario to arrange for extra protection, so he hired the local military reserves to provide their security service, and then she called her brother, Juan, to fill him in on the threat. As soon as he heard the details, he insisted on going with her. Although she was scheduled to fly with her usual team of people, he didn't want her to enter the lion's den alone, but she cut him short. "No, Juan. If anything were to happen to me, I need you to take care of the kids." She didn't let me go with her either. "Pete, you can't go because if anything happens to me, you're the one who knows what to do here." A foreboding request that would haunt my days only a year after this incident.

So it was settled. As much as we all wanted to be by her side to offer her our protection, we understood that staying back was also essential should the worse happen in Mexico. She couldn't risk not having anyone home to take care of her children and all that could ensue, and there was no turning back now. It was a done deal. Jen would be flying to Mexico the following day, as scheduled, together with her assistants Adrian and Julie, her makeup artist Jacob, and her dear friend Elena, who insisted on going with her as soon as she heard the news.

The threat had a major impact on us all. I will never forget that good-bye. It was one of the hardest ones of my life because we had no idea if it might be the last one. Her eyes were filled with fear, but Jen's mind was made up. She was going to face the beast, with faith on her side, hoping for the best while preparing for the worst.

Prior to landing in Mexico, Jen turned to her team on the jet and said, "If you don't want to go, it's okay. I won't make you go and won't think any differently of you if you decided to stay behind." But Jacob firmly replied, "No, baby, *estamos contigo hasta el fin*." *We're with you till the end*, another premonitory statement for a fate that awaited both Jen and Jacob a little more than a year later.

They landed safely in Mexico, piled out of the jet, into a bulletproof vehicle that was waiting for them, and followed the military escort to the venue. As they drove along, Jen looked out the window and saw a white cross on the side of the road. She glanced over to Julie and said, "Jules, see that white cross? That's where they got Valentín, where they killed him." An eerie silence invaded the car as they watched the cross zoom by, a pivotal moment in Jen's life that she'd pause and remember later, but now their focus was on getting this show over and done with.

They reached the venue and, while Jen was getting ready, as if they weren't already at the edge of their seats, suddenly all the lights went out, a total blackout. As they sat in the pitch-black venue, they were completely spooked, and somehow preparing for the worse. They all breathed in deeply, and as the storm rumbled outside, the lights suddenly flickered back on. Was that a sign? A bad omen? Who knew. All Jen really knew was that there was no turning back now. The show had to go on, and go on it did. Jen hit the stage that night and did her best to entertain her fans and transform the performance into a big party, something she was known for doing, but this time around she was extra vigilant. She went through the moves, toasting with the audience, trying not to raise any suspicions as she raised her glass to her lips without actually taking a drink. Relaxing into her songs and performance was impossible that night because her adrenaline was off the charts.

The concert wrapped without another hitch, the hired soldiers escorted them out of the palenque and back to the airport, and they flew back home and arrived in one piece. However, that impending threat, that life or death decision, that ride to and from the venue, the performance, they all amounted to a life-changing epiphany for Jen. The time had finally come for her to seriously reconsider her priorities and make some adjustments in her life. She had suddenly grown acutely aware of her mortality and the dangers some of these performances in Mexico posed to her life. Up until then it had been all fun and games, we'd had a great time, but now she suddenly realized that she could've actually died out there, and that was no laughing matter.

Jen always used to say, "When will my book end? When will the movie end?" referring to all the dramatic chapters in her life from which she never seemed to catch a break. However, that had been the closest call she'd ever had to staring death in the face. She'd been doing around two hundred gigs a year, if not more, she already had wealth and fame, she was tired, she yearned to be closer to her kids, and it was finally time to make that happen. It was time to leave these grueling and increasingly dangerous tours behind and open the doors to new possibilities. Yet, no matter how hard Jen tried to find some peace, the emotional roller coaster that was her life always threw her for another loop, and she still had one more ride packed with peaks and valleys to endure before her untimely death.

Chapter 9

Unforgettable Baby

Jenni Rivera ✓
@jennirivera

I'm BLESSED! I AM!

11/6/12, 4:36 AM

261 RETWEETS 266 LIKES

↩ ⇄ ♥ •••

I f you knew and loved and followed Jenni Rivera, you also know that she absolutely adored butterflies. They were everywhere. At first, I honestly thought it was kind of corny. So one day, I just had to ask, "Why a butterfly?" Never in my life did I expect such a thorough and fantastic response. First, she sent me an article to read up on them, then she said: "Did you know that before a caterpillar weaves its cocoon and begins its metamorphosis, part of the fertilization comes from manure. So basically this silk worm needs manure to survive. It needs to live in shit in order to transform into a butterfly. I think that's representative of my life because I've lived in shit. Before becoming a butterfly, I've had to live in shit in a cocoon. Only then was I able to get to where I am today."

She shut me right up with that answer and I got it. It made sense. In order to become the sensational Diva we admire to this day, she had to live and breathe a ton of shit. Oftentimes, she still felt the shit kept coming her way and made her doubt if she'd really ever made it to butterfly status. That's what made her so real to all of us who loved and admired her. From family, to friends, to employees, to fans, we all felt understood by her because she got it. Her past was far from perfect, but she owned her perfectly imperfectness and showed us that despite all that shit, it was still possible to make something of ourselves, to become our dream. At the same time, she also knew how it felt when all the cards were stacked against you and how one kind gesture, which could seem insignificant to someone else, could mean the world to you. She understood people's heartaches and pain because she'd lived through her fair share of them. She didn't just sing about the ups and downs of life. She experienced them firsthand, and that's why when her star finally rose, she wanted to share her good fortune with everyone around her.

As Jen herself used to say, "When God gives us a lot, it's our responsibility to give back." It's all the stories you've never heard, all the times she stopped what she was doing just to help her family, her friends, her loved ones, and strangers alike, behind the scenes, when the cameras were off—that's what made Jen truly unforgettable. When she hit stardom, she didn't lose herself in the glamour. She lived by those words and people loved her for that. She brought reality and relatability to the celebrity lifestyle.

Jen was very different from other celebrities, even from her own brother, Lupillo. At the height of his success, Lupillo became the guy who drove the convertible Bentley, wore five-thousand-dollar suits, smoked expensive cigars, and lived in Marina del Rey. He became an unreachable star; his fans could no longer relate to him, which in turn created a big gap between him and his audience. Meanwhile, Jen's reaction to fame was completely the opposite. The bigger her name became, the more grounded and in touch she was with her people.

She'd have dinner at her favorite local *mariscos* restaurant and pump her own gas at the station, where people who recognized her would stare in awe. "Do you think I hire someone to pump gas for my car?" she'd say, laughing, and people gobbled it up. Those interactions with Jen on a day-to-day basis were priceless for her fans. She always managed to keep it so real. She'd even go to the corner street vendor to buy a *raspado*, leaving the vendor and customers' mouths agape in admiration. "Is it really you?" they'd ask, incredulous. "Yeah, it's me," she'd say with a smile.

What was unbeknownst to many people was that Jen was still that Mexican girl from Long Beach. She never lost that part of herself to fame and fortune. It was alive and kicking and it made her who she was. Of course she had the means to go shopping in Beverly Hills and all of those high-end stores, but she honestly always felt safer among the people in the barrio. She felt at home there, it rooted her. What also didn't hurt is that she knew how to travel that fine line of communication with her fans, telling it like it is while still acknowledging their presence and love.

If she was having a meal at a restaurant and an overzealous fan approached her begging for an autograph, Jen had a way of handling the situation that calmed the person down while also allowing her to continue what she was doing. "*M'ija*, I'm really hungry," she'd say. "Just give me ten minutes to finish eating, and

I'll be sure to go over and give you a picture or whatever you need." Obviously this didn't work with everyone, but that was her, and they just had to deal with it. So, if they hounded her in the bathroom later, she'd smile and say things like, "Girl, you really wanna shake my hand now? Let me wash my hands first," which would snap the fans back to reality and remind them that she was a human being too, and it only made them love her even more. On the other hand, those that took offense, well tough shit. Jen did her best to bridge the fans' expectations of her as a celebrity by communicating and keeping it real.

That was her secret, and it worked like a charm because of Jen's unique personality. Jen had a way of saying "screw you" that made it feel like a compliment. She could call someone a *hoochie*, and that woman would feel like she had just been called a queen. It was done with so much *cariño* that it wasn't offensive. It also helped that it came from a woman who embraced her imperfections and knew she was just as beautifully flawed as everyone else.

Jen was truly just like us. She loved the simple things in life, like getting a mani-pedi, listening to music, and cooking for her family. She worked so tirelessly that these little things were the ones that brought a true smile to her face. Nothing like a day off eating frijoles with tortillas and salsita with her kids. She savored those moments like no other. And she didn't have any help. She was the one behind the stove, doing the dishes, which was another part of her life that kept her grounded. What's more, her food wasn't just reserved for her relatives. She loved to cook for her work family too. If we had an early meeting scheduled at her house, when we arrived, we'd find her in the kitchen making breakfast for us, and I'm talking about when she was already

Jenni Rivera la Gran Señora. She was just a giver by nature. She expressed her love through cooking and taking care of others; it really fed her soul.

Early on, before becoming famous, when every penny counted, she would still go out and buy costume jewelry that looked like bling-bling, and during her gigs she would give it out to her fans as a token of her appreciation for their love and support. She was spending around three hundred dollars a week on giveaway jewelry, and I thought she was crazy, but to this day, those fans who still have a piece of that jewelry cherish it as if it were the holy grail. That was Jen, it was her essence. It's not something you can teach; you're either born with it or you aren't. And Jen had it. She would literally take whatever she had on her plate and share it with you if you were hungry, so much so that she got in the habit of religiously contributing ten percent of her earnings to help others. Jen lived by faith and understood the work of God. She never preached about her Christianity because she understood how imperfect she was, but she was most definitely someone of strong faith, and giving was her church—that was her religion.

If Jen heard that a fan on his or her deathbed wanted to meet her, she didn't go to a Make a Wish Foundation or any other organization to make a donation. She would carve out time and personally make her way to the hospital to see that person. And once there, it wasn't a quick in-and-out visit or a media opportunity. She would sit by them, pray, talk, sing. She made sure she gave that person love and made sure they were well taken care of before she resumed her busy schedule and life. I can't tell you the countless amounts of personal hospital visits and checks she wrote for fans in need, be it a cancer patient or a parent who had just lost a child. The key, what made her even more beloved by her fans, was that she didn't just donate money. She also always made a point to donate her precious time.

And it was no secret she had a soft spot for older people, single mothers, and children because she couldn't imagine seeing her parents or kids suffering in any which way, and she knew firsthand what it meant to be a single parent in this world. As Julie, her assistant, once said to me, "The Children's Hospital of Los Angeles (CHLA) was probably one of Jenni's favorite places to visit. She felt at home there. She was given the freedom to go wherever she wanted, and she would pop into the children's rooms and surprise them. The smile of every child she saw truly reflected on her face—the smile, the look in her eyes, the sense of fulfillment, the warmth in her heart—she always left CHLA renewed. No matter what she was going through, she found new appreciation for life in that hospital." And it didn't stop at hospitals.

Back when she was on set filming *Filly Brown*, Jen overheard that the wife of the movie's backstage photographer, John Castillo, an older Mexican-American man who was there donating his time for the project, was battling cancer. When she got wind of this, before leaving the set, she pulled him aside and said, "I want you to know that I'm donating my paycheck to you and your wife. Good luck with her fight against cancer." Later, when John heard Jen passed away, he was one of the many people who reached out to me, saying he'd never forget that act of kindness. No one had ever done such a thing for him in his lifetime. Those were the things that made her unforgettable. These unpublicized private moments happened throughout her life, and she wasn't bragging about all this; she simply did it from her heart. No one can even imagine the many fans Jen helped bury, in silence, with no media stunts or attention. She paid for their funerals, paid for their remains to be taken back to Mexico, and helped with whatever the families needed to give their loved one peace and find some sense of closure.

I experienced this act of kindness firsthand. When my mom passed away from cancer, Jen not only dedicated an award she won at a show here in L.A. to my mother, she also contributed to my mother's funeral service. I didn't ask her for this, but she insisted, saying, "Let me help you." That was her. She was always there. Now, hold up, you didn't have to be sick to get Jen's help. She helped many others too, visiting fans who were going through a rough patch and giving them cash as gifts to help them out. She also gave out wheelchairs, cars, participated in telethons, radio fundraisers, and any other giving venture that could benefit those in need.

Another priceless moment etched in my mind as a perfect example of her understanding and generosity happened at one of her gigs in Mexico. Sometimes the venues she played had fairs set up outside with vendors selling different kinds of merchandise. This one time, we saw a local artist who was selling Jenni Rivera keychains and buttons; in other words, he was selling unauthorized Jenni Rivera merchandise using her image on products without permission. If another artist would've seen this, he or she would've flipped out and had the merchant's post immediately shut down, but that sure as hell wasn't Jen. She was compassionate because she understood him. She knew he was doing this to feed his family. She herself had done the same thing years ago as a teenager in Long Beach. So rather than report him or have him shut down his little business, she simply rolled down the window, poked her head out, and asked him how much the merchandise cost.

When the man looked up, he turned pale and silent, as if he'd just seen God. I think he was preparing for her to let him have it, so he started handing over his product to her, but she quickly stopped him. "No, no, just tell me how much it costs, because I want to buy it all." Baffled, he told her the price, and she replied, "Okay, I'm going to buy it, but I want you to go and give away each piece of merchandise to my fans, for free, on my behalf. And I'm sending my team over to make sure you do this." The man had a look of disbelief on his face that was priceless, and he followed her orders to a tee. Jen just got it, she never forgot what that struggle felt like, she never forgot how hard it was to go through life with nothing but the shirt on your back, and that's what made her unforgettable.

Her generosity didn't stop at hospitals and on the streets. Her donations and care reached her family and friends as well. She loved seeing people succeed, especially family and friends. She not only gave many of her loved ones money to help them out of a tough spot, she went even further. She'd pay for medical procedures too. It came to a point where we had a running joke in the team: you weren't really loved by Jenni unless you went under the knife because of her. So, if she loved you and she found out you wanted a boob job, Jen would make arrangements and pay for it. She'd cover liposuctions, facelifts, you name it. She did it to me too. At one point, when I was at my heaviest, weighing close to four hundred pounds and suffering from diabetes, Jen looked me in the eye and said, "I'm not going to lose you. I need you around." Without even asking, she followed that with, "So you're going to go have a gastric sleeve done in Mexico." Shocked, I simply said,

"What?" to which she replied matter-of-factly, "Yeah, we leave tomorrow." And that was that.

Another person Jen helped was her grandmother from Sonora, Mexico. That señora was a real trip! She liked to drink beer, talk shit about men and sex, and dance. It was basically Jen at seventy-plus years. And Jen adored her NaNa—that was her mama in every sense. She was fantastic, delightful, always the life of the party, speaking her mind, and making Jen's friends cry with laughter. Like the rest of the family, she'd also lived a hard life, so when Jen finally made it big, she set up an account for her abuela in Mexico and religiously deposited money into it every single month. Jen wanted to make sure that her NaNa spent the rest of her days on earth taken care of and pampered, always having access to whatever she needed. That's why it was so heartbreaking to see how, when Jen passed away, with no regard to what she would've wanted, the family went and cut that account. A year later, their NaNa passed away, destitute, in a county facility in Sonora. The situation was so bad that it was even a struggle to have her buried. Lupillo had to address the family in order to give her the burial she deserved. Definitely not the end Jen would've wanted for her dear abuela; had she been alive, she would've been devastated to see such an outcome … had she been alive, it wouldn't have happened.

As Jen became more powerful with her fans, many local and national politicians took notice and started turning to her for support. Jen had her finger on the pulse of the Latino community, she was approachable, she was always in touch with her people, and she was considered an important community leader. Before we knew it, Jen was lending herself to help some politicians who in turn would help her people, and even managed to get some officials elected, but she wasn't really receiving anything in return.

As I observed this, I reached out to her one day and suggested we hire a political consultant. "Listen, we saw this play out in the black community with Magic Johnson and a local L.A. politician with urban redevelopment," I said to Jen. I had worked with Magic Johnson prior to working with her. "Why don't we emulate the same structure in the Latino community?" I suggested. I kept thinking, *Why couldn't we get an Oscar de la Hoya or a Jenni Rivera to help develop our communities too? Why couldn't we have a woman's shelter funded by the local government and have Jen participate in this giving venture?* It was a perfect fit, something she was passionate about, and something that made her happy. She loved being able to give back to her community, so it was time to take a more serious step to make it happen. That's when we scheduled a meeting with political consultant James Acevedo, the Godfather of Latino Politics in Southern California.

We met for breakfast at Jen's house, discussed the projects we wanted to get off the ground, and James became our point person, working closely with other community leaders and politicians to make some noticeable progress. Jen was wrapping up her album *Mi vida loca*, and was really excited about using her rising celebrity star for good causes. So we began to pursue these plans aggressively, studying what Emilio Estefan had done in Miami, and figuring out what we could apply to what we were trying to do in California. The idea wasn't to turn Jen into a real estate tycoon. It was more about learning how to use her fame wisely to bring new opportunities to the community.

Jen wanted to create real business opportunities for people within fields that they could excel in. It was all about keeping it real and accessible. Most Latinas have some specialty—like sewing or cooking, for example—so our idea was to take these basic skills into account and teach them how to use them in their favor to build a business. Jen loved this idea because she knew that giving them a business skill, something with which they could make their own money, would also in turn give them the financial freedom needed to leave abusive relationships, fend for themselves and their children, and make something of themselves. She knew all too well how important it was to have this independence. Many women who solely depend on their husbands or boyfriends don't leave their abusive partners because they simply don't have the means to do so. Not only that, many women don't even know where to begin to find those means, they don't know where to start or how to make it happen, so they end up stuck in these life-threatening situations with nowhere to turn.

Jen knew from personal experience that regardless of whether you are in a good or abusive relationship, every woman should have her own side money to contribute to the household and to have a way out if it ever comes to that. So why not create a place that offers this possibility to these women in need? That's where Jen's head was at. She wanted to use her pull as a celebrity and combine it with local politicians and their resources to make it happen. It was a sound plan, the people we reached out to were on board, and it was all in the works.

We were planning redevelopment projects, looking into affordable housing and how to bring these ideas to the Latino community, but then 2008 came around, the housing market crashed, and everything was stalled due to the severe financial crisis. Everyone around Jen was affected by the housing market crash, even her brother. It really hit home, so the redevelopment plans were put on hold; the focus now shifted on everyone who had been affected by this crisis.

In 2009, Jen moved to Encino and got involved with New Economics for Women (NEW). Her plan was to turn her old seven-bedroom Corona home into a woman's shelter. However, she got quite a bit of pushback from her neighbors. When Jen lived there, the neighbors assumed that her expensive cars and tour buses and genre of music were all tied to cartels. They assumed she was some type of female drug lord, so when she moved away, they were happy, and she knew getting their vote to turn her old home into a women's shelter would be nearly impossible, so she decided to look for other opportunities to make this happen.

Meanwhile, never one to sit still, when 2010 came along, during some downtime between tours where we were all on vacation, Jen suddenly said, "Guys, we're extending our vacation this year so we can all go down to Arizona." She wanted us to join the community in Phoenix, Arizona, and march against the SB 1070 Law, a legislative act that was being voted on, which, if passed, would be one of the strictest and broadest anti-immigration laws in many years. So we loaded up the tour bus, took our families along for the ride, and drove down to Arizona to protest with our fellow Latinos. It was a three-mile march under the Arizona sun, but that didn't stop Jen from walking side-by-side everyone else in Phoenix.

She didn't skip the march and meet us at the finish line, no way. She was right there, we all were, marching together with our families and the Arizona communities, joining forces and supporting one another during this critical time. It was exhilarating. And guess what? There were no cameras following her while we marched, and she wasn't doing it as a publicity stunt. It was a genuine act of solidarity, concern, and support. That was Jen.

As our work with James Acevedo continued to progress, aside from using her support in the community wisely, we were working on organizing her generosity to make the most of her giving nature. Up until then, Jen made donations to shelters and hospitals and individuals straight out of her own pocket. She didn't have any corporate sponsors or anyone else backing her charity. If someone needed a car, Jen would go and buy it with her own checkbook. She was all about taking action, and that was solid gold, but I explained to her that as a celebrity, she could actually have a car manufacturer donate a car in her name without having to dive into her own earnings. There were better ways to structure her need to give and help others. She was okay with that idea, but made one thing crystal clear from the get-go: if she was going to give something to a person in need or an organization, it had to come from her, not someone else or another company. And that's how the idea of the Jenni Rivera Love Foundation came to be. We discussed everything we could accomplish through her own foundation, and she was all in. "Set it up," she said, and we went to work.

Jen's goal for her foundation was to offer scholarships to young women who worked hard and hoped to continue their educations. And I'm not talking just college or university scholarships. I'm talking trade schools too. Jen wanted to help

women and families in need succeed, and in some cases it came
down to simply learning a trade to help them get off of welfare.
She wanted to provide that leg up life hadn't afforded them; she
hoped to make a real difference in their life. And she wasn't about
to take any type of salary to do this. This was pure charity, giving,
what made Jen happy, what made her whole. Nowadays, many
nonprofits are structured to pay their founders salaries, and some
use it as another form of income, but that sure as hell was not Jen.
She was adamant about having her nonprofit organization be
exactly that: not for profit. One hundred percent of the proceeds
were destined to help women and families in need. She wanted it
all to go back to the community, her people.

As with many of her other ventures, it took us around two
years to make it happen, but it was finally up and running prior
to her accident. Since then, it's had its fair share of struggles,
including a recent suspension, but it has now been reinstated
and seems like it might survive. I hope it does. This is a huge part
of Jen's legacy, and I know it would've made her ecstatic to see it
thrive.

The same year we began planning the Jenni Rivera Love
Foundation, Jen was also named spokeswoman for the National
Coalition Against Battered Women and Domestic Violence in Los
Angeles. It was in honor of her ongoing fight for women's rights,
the protection of children subject to abuse, and her constant
dedication to protecting battered women everywhere. On that
same day in 2010, the LA City Council officially named August 6
Jenni Rivera Day to commemorate her work and involvement in
the community.

That was the epitome of the Jen that I knew. Sure, she was
a crazy *cabrona* sometimes, tough as nails when she had to be.

If I had hair, I would've lost it all working by her side with all the ups and downs we journeyed through together, but she was also always incredibly gracious and kind. And at the end of the day, all she really wanted was to give her family, friends, and community the love and loyalty she so yearned to have in her own personal life.

Chapter 10

Happily Ever After?
Love, Loss, and Betrayals

jennirivera
@jennirivera

Recientemente perdi a 4 personas muy
importantes en mi vida...pero al
conocer a las personas nuevas que he
conocido, vivir el cariño y apoyo de
mis amigos y equipo....volver a abrazar
a quienes hace mucho no estaban en mi
vida...estar mas cerca de mi familia...y
sentir el calor de mi publico como
nunca antes....las volveria a perder una
y otra vez. I'm okay. #lifegoeson

2012-11-18

After her relationship with Fernando officially ended in 2007, Jen had lovers and booty calls, but it seemed no one would be able to fill that void until she met Esteban ... or so she thought. Fernando was her muse, her soul mate, her everything, but their relationship was tumultuous, and his addiction prevented them from having their "happily ever after." She wasn't sure if she could ever really love again, until she fell for Esteban, a man whom she believed would finally be able to provide her with the stability she and her kids needed.

Jen met Esteban Loaiza at one of her palenque concerts in Mazatlán, Mexico, on December 7, 2008. Gabo was actually the one who introduced them that night, not knowing he was introducing Jen to her future husband. Esteban was a successful baseball player who had recently played for the LA Dodgers, a true sports hero in Mexico. She was la Gran Señora, la Diva de la Banda, the one and only Jenni Rivera. It seemed like a match made in heaven.

Initially, aside from finding him physically attractive, what drew Jen to Esteban was that he appeared to be a successful man, someone who had made it, a guy who had his shit together and wouldn't need Jen to come to the rescue, someone who could finally take care of her for a change. He began courting her with lavish gifts and grand gestures, and she allowed herself to be wooed. This was a first for Jen. She'd never been treated like a queen before. Esteban came into Jen's life with his fancy jewelry, cool cars, and expensive clothes and did all in his power to sweep her off her feet. He'd buy her five pairs of jeans, a pair of shoes a week; he enjoyed the finer things in life and opened her up to this possibility, something new and exciting to Jen. She'd never been pampered by a man like this before; she was used to being the provider for everyone, so, although it was somewhat overwhelming for her, it was also a definite breath of fresh air.

To top it off, Esteban was a calm, stable, agreeable guy who shied away from confrontations, someone who represented what Jen had come to believe she needed in her life. Yes, she was attracted to him, but in all honesty, neither Gabo nor I believe she was ever head over heels in love with him. We'd seen her experience an all-consuming and profound love with Fernando, and this was very different. To her, Esteban represented the ideal husband and father to her children, a man who could provide warmth and stability, someone who didn't need her money because he had his own, a decent guy and good father figure. She knew she'd made extremely bad choices in her previous relationships, and she wanted to get it right this time. It wasn't really about being in love. It was about evolving to a more mature chapter in her life for the sake of her children and her parents, who hoped to see her settle down with a good guy for a change.

Jen thought Esteban was the right choice, but it wasn't a choice that necessarily filled her with joy. It was more about what she was supposed to do, kind of pitting la Gran Señora against the Diva. La Gran Señora was responsible, she made sound decisions, and chose stability over love. La Diva was passionate, she let her heart guide her, and love would conquer all in her world. In this case, La Gran Señora was winning, at least for now.

A month after meeting, they made their relationship public. I always thought it was a bit rushed, but Jen seemed so in love with the idea of this perfect man that she didn't want to wait it out. She just went ahead and took the plunge. As they found their footing as a couple in 2009, unexpected tragedy hit Jenni's family: death came knocking on the door.

Jenni Rivera's Ex-Husband Dies

Even though their divorce hadn't been pretty, once the dust settled, Jen made sure to maintain a good relationship with Juan Lopez for the sake of their kids, and that meant not only communicating with him, but also taking them to visit him in prison after his sentence. In 2009, Juan had been serving year two of his ten-year prison sentence when he was suddenly afflicted with pneumonia. As soon as Jen heard about his condition, she moved mountains to get him transferred to a hospital to receive proper treatment. However, by the time he arrived at the hospital, he had begun suffering complications due to the infection, and his health quickly deteriorated. It wasn't looking good for Juan, so Jen made sure to take her kids to the hospital to see him and be with him, and she even sat by his side, singing to him on what was quickly becoming his deathbed. Jen was tough but she had a heart of gold. She didn't forget, but she was big on forgiveness, especially if you owned up to your mistakes, because she knew that she wasn't perfect either. That's why she was able to remain by Juan's bedside wholeheartedly in this time of need.

Those first two weeks in July were agonizing. Jen wanted to keep the faith, but she could see Juan was only getting worse, until finally, on July 14, 2009, she got the dreaded call. We were in a white hummer limousine coming back from Delano, California, where a high school arts department had just been named in Jen's honor. I was there with her together with Esteban and her kids. It was a celebratory day that suddenly took a tragic turn. María, Juan's sister, was on the other line when Jen answered her phone. As Jen listened to María, her expression changed instantly. She looked at me, then she quickly glanced at her kids, and I knew something was wrong. "Okay, I'll call you as soon as I get home. We're almost home, we're almost home," Jen said, right before hanging up. "It's Juan," she whispered to me, and I got it. Then, she gathered herself and observed her children, as they continued celebrating the day and laughing, knowing that what she had to tell them would change their lives forever. Juan Lopez had passed away. Jenicka and Johnny no longer had a father on this earth.

The Big Engagement and Its Pitfalls

As Jen helped her children mourn Juan Lopez's sudden passing, her relationship with Esteban continued to flourish. By January 2010, a year after they met, they were engaged. Esteban had carefully planned this moment so that he could pop the question in front of the people Jen loved the most on this planet: her children. They had all gone out to dinner that night together, and as they sat around the table, satisfied by the delicious meal and about ready to dig into their dessert, Esteban took a deep breath and launched into his big speech. He looked around at everyone and said that he wanted to be a part of their family. The children glanced excitedly at their mom, who, oblivious to what was about to go down, kept chowing down on her dessert. Then suddenly, Esteban turned to Jen and said, "Baby, if I were to ask you to marry me, would you say yes?" And she replied, "Yeah," without taking her eyes off the plate, still unaware that he was going for it right then and there. Her children stood up and started clapping, he fell on one knee, and she suddenly dropped her fork and turned toward him, finally getting the picture of what he was trying to do. Tears began streaming down her face as she saw the box in his hands, but she was so caught off guard, she didn't give him an immediate answer. Realizing she still hadn't uttered a word, her kids said, "Mother, say yes!" and she snapped back to reality and blurted out, "I said yes," and they all burst into celebration. When she later recounted this story to María Celeste on the show *Al Rojo Vivo*, she poignantly said, "I didn't know what to say," and then followed it with, "Well, I wasn't going to say no." Jen was shocked, moved, she'd never seen a ring like that, she'd never been proposed to before, but ultimately it was clear that her "Yes" was more for her kids than for herself.

Esteban had managed to sweep her off her feet, and they were married within two years of meeting, but the relationship was not without its premarital glitches. After the engagement came their first big crisis as well as red flags that we should've paid closer attention to, but we didn't because he really seemed like the whole package. Jen and those of us closest to her honestly thought he had his shit together, but much to our dismay, we'd soon be proved wrong.

As they jumped into wedding planning mode, Jen was taken aback when Esteban's mother asked her to sign a prenup. It bothered her somewhat because she was a self-made woman, took great pride in her work and making her own way in this world, and was far from money hungry, but she went with the flow and agreed. One day, as they reviewed different drafts of the prenup at her house, Jen was utterly shocked and dismayed by what she discovered.

"Hey, this draft says you have a daughter in San Diego. Why didn't you ever mention that to me?" asked Jen, baffled, hoping it was some sort of mistake, unable to wrap her head around not knowing such an important fact about the man she was about to marry.

"It's not like she's in my life. It was just a fling I had early in my career. I send her money, but it's not like she's my daughter," he said nonchalantly.

Jen's heart dropped to the floor. She couldn't believe what she was hearing. It was one thing to find out he had a daughter through a prenup, but his quick dismissal of her existence was completely outrageous and unacceptable. She looked at him in disbelief and called me and her friend Elena, asking that we come over ASAP. Tears were spilling out of her eyes when I arrived. She hugged me and sobbed bitterly. Once Elena arrived, she took us to where Esteban was sitting and, pointing toward us, glared at him and yelled, "Tell them, you piece of shit!" My first reaction when I heard her say that, the first thought that crossed my mind, was, *If he laid a hand on her, Imma gonna screw him over.* Dumbfounded by her reaction, he quietly explained that he had fathered a child early in his career and never told her or us about his daughter.

"How can I marry the man that I have spent my entire career criticizing and defending women from? It goes against everything I stand for! I can't marry him!" Jen wailed.

Esteban did everything in his power to make his actions sound logical, but to no avail. They broke up then and there. It seemed like that would be the end of their relationship for good, but it wasn't. A short time later, they met at Elena's birthday party and spent the entire night talking it all out, so much so that Jen missed a morning interview she had scheduled with Raul Molina from the show *El Gordo y la Flaca*. As the sun rose, and a new day came to light, they had managed to reconcile.

The wedding was officially back on, but Jen still wasn't completely sold on marrying him. Gabo recalls a particular incident that made her sentiment crystal clear. They were at a hotel in Chihuahua, Mexico, after one of Jen's performances. Gabo's room was right next to theirs and, as Gabo was getting ready for bed, Jen's sudden loud and angry voice caught his attention. She was arguing with Esteban. "But why did you do that? Why did you make me look bad? Why?!?", she shouted furiously. She continued going at him, stronger by the minute, the argument escalating to a full-blown fight until she finally exploded, "And you know what? Grab your checkbook because I'm not going to spend a dime on the wedding! I don't want to get married. Do you hear me? I don't want to get married! My children are the ones who are excited about this wedding, not me! So grab your checkbook because I don't want to pay for any of it. If you're so crazy about getting married, then you pay for it! I don't want to get married! If I do, it's just to give my children a father, but not because I want a husband, got it?" Gabo was shocked at what he overheard. He knew Jen wasn't madly in love with Esteban, as did I, but he hadn't heard her express herself so adamantly about it before. Suffice to say they eventually made up and the wedding was still on, but it was a far cry from an honest and joyful engagement.

Nevertheless, Esteban and Jen went on to have their nationally televised fairy tale wedding on September 8, 2010, without a hitch. What no one knew was that earlier that day, while flying on the chopper that was transporting her to the venue, in a moment of clarity and panic, she picked up her cell phone and dialed Fernando's number.

"Guess what?" she said when he picked up. "I'm getting married!"

Fernando didn't believe her, he laughed it off, thinking she was just bullshitting him as always, so she said it again.

"I'm on my way to get married."

It was Jen's one small cry for help to the man she was still emotionally attached to, the one she felt was her soul mate, someone she would never forget, even though she knew she couldn't be with him. But nothing came of that call. He honestly thought it was a joke, so he did nothing, which he regrets to this day. He wishes he would've believed her. If he had, he would've totally tried to talk her out of it, but that's not what happened. As she hung up and put her cell phone away, Jen dismissed any doubts from her mind, gathered herself, stepped out of the chopper, and headed to her so-called "happily ever after."

The wedding was perfect, she seemed like she was glowing with joy, and every one of us believed she was finally getting the happy ending she so yearned for and deserved, completely unaware of the debacle she would have to face only two years later. However, before her husband's charade crumbled before her eyes, another drama was about to unravel, this time involving her son, Mikey.

Jenni Rivera's Son Arrested for Having Sex with a Minor!

As was common in Jen's bittersweet life, every happy moment, each celebration, was somehow always followed by a dramatic turn of events. When Jen and Esteban got married, everyone was allowed to bring a guest to the wedding. Mikey chose to invite a longtime friend from Corona, who in turn asked him if it was cool if he also brought his aunt and cousin. When Mikey checked in with Jen to see if that was okay, she said, "Sure, no problem," so they were all set. At the wedding Mikey and his friend's cousin hit it off, they talked for a while, and finally decided to exchange numbers and stay in touch.

The wedding came and went and everyone went back to their own lives, except for Mikey and this girl, who continued texting, talking, and making plans to hang out again. They finally set a date, and Mikey drove over to Corona to see her. They spent a while together, messed around, and had consensual sex. Then, days turned into weeks, and this casual hookup began to fizzle, so Mikey turned his attention elsewhere. Upset, the girl ran to her mom to tell her what had happened, and they came up with a plan. First, the girl's mother had her take a DIY rape kit so they could accuse him of rape. Then, the mom contacted Mikey directly and began threatening him. Here's the clincher: the girl was around sixteen years old, and Mikey had just turned nineteen, so technically, even though they were still both teenagers, he was past his eighteenth birthday and now considered an adult. So the mom had the perfect ammunition. She not only threatened to press charges for raping her daughter, but also for having sex with a minor.

Scared shitless by the sudden accusations, Mikey turned to his sister, Chiquis, for help. Chiquis quickly stepped up to the plate and tried to talk some sense into the mom, who finally showed her true colors: she said she wouldn't file any charges if Jenni paid them $300,000 and helped her daughter with her musical career. Now, stuck between a rock and a hard place and unable to respond to such a request, Chiquis had no choice but to get Jenni involved. After filling her in, Jen called Mikey into her office and blurted out, "What the hell did you do?" If Mikey had really done something wrong, Jen was ready to let his ass rot in jail.

"You tell me what happened, and don't you dare lie to me, you hear me?!"

"No, Mom, it wasn't like that at all," said Mikey, terrified, and he went on to explain it all play by play and showed her the text messages to back up his story.

I had been sitting in the office all along, as Jen and I had been in the middle of a business meeting when the shit hit the fan. As

I watched Mikey tell his side of the story to Jen, Chiquis walked back into the office, cell phone in hand, and tells Jen the girl's mother called back and was on the line. Mama Bear Jen grabbed that phone and took control of the situation in one fell swoop.

"Hi, how are you? This is Jenni Rivera, Mikey's mom. So, what's going on?" Jen listened patiently, then replied, "If anything has happened to your daughter, I will make sure that she gets all the help and treatment that she needs. If she was taken advantage of by my son, I will make sure to help her. But there's no way you can put a price on your daughter's mental well-being. Asking me for this money sounds a lot like blackmail to me. If you think you're going to get a dollar out of me this way, then I think you're better off filing charges and we'll have our day in court."

As time went by, we figured the problem had gone away, until one morning Mikey was arrested in Corona. Anthony Lopez, Jen's lawyer, and I went to bail him out, while the media, which was already swarming the place, had a field day plastering his photo across their platforms, and comparing him to his father, since he too had had sex with minors. It got real ugly real fast, and the whole thing shook the family to the core. Jen knew her son wasn't innocent—he did have sex with this girl—but he was far from the monster the media was making him out to be. She was once again devastated.

Ultimately having faith helped Jen through this event. She prayed, she cried, she gathered the strength she needed to prevail, and she went to court with her head held high, and Mikey by her side, prepared to go to war for her kid, but with great faith that justice would be served. In the end, the truth conquered all. Even though it was finally agreed that the sex was consensual and not rape, he was technically still an adult in the eye of the court and she was a minor, so the case could not be dismissed, but they managed to strike a deal. Mikey was put on probation with no jail time, but there was absolutely no financial gain by the other party, and Jen once again had defended her family and herself victoriously.

It was hard for Jen to understand why people acted with such malice in their hearts, going to such lengths to take advantage of her because she never saw herself as the big celebrity she had become. She always remained grounded, and that was part of her beautiful essence. It was part of her magic as a human being. The trial helped her open her eyes to her kids' reality. She suddenly realized they had been living a very sheltered life, and it was time to teach them some responsibility. So, aside from being on probation, she got Mikey a job as a dishwasher at a seafood restaurant. It was time for a reality check, and she wasn't afraid to give it to him. After the dishwashing stint, she had him working as a valet parking attendant. That was Jenni all the way, learning from life's lessons and doing all she could to make sure her children grew up understanding the value of a dollar, something she thought Esteban knew, but man was she still in for a big surprise.

A Dwindling Marriage

Jen took marriage very seriously. As rebellious as she was in many aspects of her life, she was also quite the traditional lady. She would never intentionally mess with a married man, and as a married woman she knew she wouldn't break that marital vow. But goodness was she ever conflicted. On one hand, she thought that this was what she needed, someone stable for her and the kids. She saw how happy we all were for her, rooting for that fairy-tale marriage she so deserved, so she carried on. It was for the best, or so she thought, something she was supposed to do; however, her heart and soul were dying a slow and tedious death. The man lacked passion, ambition, drive, and that was quietly killing Jen inside, but she continued to play the part of the good wife.

Hoping to spark that go-getter she fooled herself into believing Esteban had in him, Jen came to me many times asking me to find him some work, be it a baseball clinic, working with city youth, anything to keep him active. Jen thrived on the hustle and when she married Esteban, she thought he was a hustler like her, but it turned out he was a total homebody. He liked waking up late, while Jen had always been an early-morning riser. To Jen late was 6:00 a.m., so waking up at 11:00 a.m. was just unacceptable. These little things started to add up and get under her skin.

We're talking about a woman who was bursting with creativity and energy, who had a slew of businesses launching or running simultaneously and was always one step ahead of the rest of us. This was also a woman who once said in an interview that she liked that she was marrying someone who could be there to support her should she ever have to stop working, not that she wanted to or would, but it was nice to know she could lean on someone for a change. Jenni saw him as a stereotypical jock, doubted his ability to express himself clearly, and sometimes thought he was as dumb as a bag of rocks, and Jen began to resent him big time. She suddenly realized that one of her main issues with Esteban was that she honestly felt no sense of admiration for him, and she confessed this to Gabo after observing him with his girlfriend. "I can tell your girlfriend is impressed by you, you're her everything, someone she looks up to. And you know what? I don't feel like that about

Esteban. I see him and I'm honestly not that proud of him when we're out and about."

Ultimately, Jen began to feel betrayed. The image he had portrayed when he was trying to sweep her off her feet had now crumbled into a reality that was quite opposite to the man whom she initially thought had all his shit together and was up to par with her ethics in work and life. I honestly believe that the toughest issue Jen had to face time and again throughout her life wasn't welfare or poverty, but rather deception, in all its shapes and forms and all its ugly glory. Little did she know she was now on the cusp of the ultimate chain of deception and disappointment from four of her closest people. Her inner circle of trust was about to implode before her eyes and ultimately swallow her in pain and shatter our so-called unbreakable diva into a million little pieces.

Gabriel "Gabo" Vázquez

Gabriel Vázquez was a huge part of Jen's life. He was not only her road manager, but also someone who outlasted each and every one of her marriages. She used to say this about both of us. We were the men she'd had steadily by her side for the longest amount of time, her brothers, her yin and yang, the two men she could turn to for strength and balance in her life. If she needed to feel protected, she'd head over to me, and if she needed someone to comfort her, it was Gabo she went to. He made her laugh and feel good, he was nurturing and kind. Jen and Gabo spent endless hours on the road together. He was the one who made sure she ate, she woke up on time, she had everything she needed; he'd been there for her through thick and thin, comforting her through all the tears and celebrating all her successes. This was someone she felt safe with, so losing him was a truly gut-wrenching moment in Jen's life.

When I came on board the team, Jen and Gabo had already been in the trenches together, touring in a van, working their asses off to make something of her career. However, as time passed, he became a constant target and a continuous suspect within Jen's inner circle. People were always suggesting that he might be swiping money from her tour income, starting with Lupillo, who was the first to plant that seed of doubt in her mind. "Be careful with him. He is stealing from you," he'd say to her. Not one to stay quiet, Jen would ask Gabo, and time after time, he'd defend himself and prove his innocence. He endured years of bullshit, but was always a steadfast figure by Jen's side, the one who remained positive and upbeat when the cards were stacked against her, the person who believed in her when others were slamming doors in her face, the one who protected her dream and persevered with her to make it a reality.

However, in 2011 things came to a screeching and unexpected end, costing Jen and Gabo not only their business relationship, but their many years of friendship. This time around, it started with the seed of doubt planted by Esteban. He had Jen's ear now, and he kept whispering into it, causing her to suspect her old friend and loyal road manager. I honestly think Esteban was hoping to become the next Juan Lopez. He wanted that role as manager, and in order to get it, he needed Gabo out of the way. It was a clear grab for power, and Esteban seized his chance with a pair of invoices that just didn't add up. It was now or never. He put the paperwork he'd come across inside a manila envelope and handed it to Jen as obvious proof of Gabo's wrongdoings.

When Jen opened it, as she read through the invoices over and over again, she finally called me and asked that I come to her office. As soon as I walked through the doorway, she handed me the envelope and simply asked me to take a look at the paperwork inside. I sat down and started reading through the documents, staring at the numbers on one page and the numbers on another, baffled as to why they didn't add up. I recognized the information: it was an invoice for a show in Mexico. Actually there were two practically identical invoices, but one had more money coming in than the other.

"What's this?" I asked Jen, confused.

"Looks like what people have been saying all these years is true," she said, quickly jumping to the conclusion that the missing money that she hadn't received had been swiped by Gabo.

What were we supposed to think? When comparing Gabo's version of the invoice with Jen's final version, there were clearly 200,000 pesos missing from her final payment. Where did they go? Why had he never mentioned this sum to her? Why were there two versions of this invoice? It was easy to assume that it must've been Gabo taking a cut for himself, especially after years of hearing these suspicions from people around her.

"What the hell?!" I blurted out. "What are you going to do?"

They had a weekend tour coming up, so Jen had Gabo over for dinner and conducted business as usual with him that evening. She made brown rice and salmon, they went over the last details for their upcoming tour, and when he left, as he kissed her granddaughter Jaylah good-bye, Jen felt a pang in her heart, knowing that it would be the last time he would be there with them. She could barely look him in the eye, knowing all too well that her eyes just couldn't lie.

The weekend came along and they went to Mexico as planned. Once the shows were over, she called Gabo over to the pool where she was sunbathing and handed him the manila envelope. As he went through it, his face dropped, and she simply asked, "Why?"

That was the key question, the one question, which if answered, could've cleared his name once again of all suspicion, but this time he chose to remain quiet. And it wasn't guilt that silenced him; it was fear for his life and Jenni's. His silence was the only thing that would guarantee their protection, but it also cost him their friendship and his job.

After Gabo and Jen's years of tireless work in Mexico, Jen had finally become La Gran Señora, but that title also came with risks. Mexico is known as cartel country. No matter how hard the government works to keep cartels at bay, they still have the last say in many areas of Mexico, and when doing business there, it's nearly impossible not to run into them eventually. Gabo was from Mexico, he'd done business there for years, so he knew how to navigate this ship well. It was a very delicate matter, but somehow he made it work without putting anyone in danger. Only after Jen's passing did I hear Gabo's version of this debacle, and it all finally made sense to me. He's been silent long enough. The time has come for him to take the page and explain how it all went down in his own words:

In Mexico the law of the land is mainly enforced by the cartels. Their power and influence are so great that their wishes are usually everyone else's command, and that includes being able to safely play music in many of the big venues throughout the country. Once Jenni became

La Gran Señora and started playing larger sites, it was our turn to abide by the cartels' rules. In our case, it was all about the kickbacks, a fee the cartels charged the promoters in exchange for keeping the artists safe in their territory. If the promoters were trying to organize any type of event, the cartels would reach out and tell them they required a cut to ensure everyone's safety. So the promoters, in turn, would reach out to the artists' teams to share this extraordinary "fee," and we had no choice but to accept it and include it as another tour expense. If we didn't, we wouldn't be able to have our artist play those venues, or he or she would perform at their own risk. A risk I wasn't willing to take for Jenni. A rumor about all this started circling among the bigger artists and eventually it reached Jenni. "Oye, Gabo, they don't ask us for anything, right?" she asked me, addressing the rumor. And I said no. But that wasn't true. We'd already been paying these kickbacks for a while when she came to me with this question, but I had decided not to say anything to her to avoid much bigger problems.

Everyone knew that no one messed with Jenni. When she heard this rumor, aside from asking me about it, she went off and also said, "You better make sure you never give those criminals a cent of my money. That money belongs to my kids, not to those damn thugs."

"I know, Jenni. I know," I replied, knowing full well that this was exactly what we were doing in order for her to continue playing and growing her fan base. First off, I didn't want to tell her because I didn't want to scare her with all of this. I was taking care of it, and she didn't have

*to worry about those things. Second, it was also part
of the cartels' request. As much as they respected her,
they also knew she had a tendency to use social media
to rant about whatever or whoever had pissed her off.
And they had no interest in having their cartel names
splashed all over the media and associated with charging
artists kickbacks, even though that was exactly what was
happening in real life.*

*So, on one hand, Jen didn't want me paying them a
cent to play at those venues, and on the other, they'd been
explicitly clear that if word got out publicly that they were
involved, our lives would be on the line. It was as simple as
that. And I knew that if Jenni found out, that was it. There
was no way she wouldn't tweet about it and talk about it
publicly because that was who she was. She wouldn't take
anyone's crap, no matter how dangerous or powerful they
were, so keeping this from her was not only allowing her to
play in our beloved Mexico, but also protecting her and me
from life-threatening consequences.*

*And for a while, it worked. We paid up and no one
bothered us. Sure, we always had an escort and drove
around in an SUV once Jenni was famous and playing
around Mexico, but our security team was basically there
to help us with her adoring fans; they didn't carry weapons
or anything of the sort. It was the kickback that guaranteed
our safety. If we didn't pay to play, we could've easily been
mugged or worse. It was our only way to guarantee our safe
passage in those territories. I learned early on that the best
way to handle these payments was through the promoters.
I was told by other colleagues that it was best if the cartels*

never saw me or spoke to me directly. That's how all the other managers for big-name artists were handling this, so I followed suit.

However, even though I knew I was protecting her, not being upfront about it all with Jenni came back to haunt me in the end. That day, when she confronted me with those two invoices and questioned me about the missing money—which was the exact amount of the kickback for that show—I knew it was all over.

"Why did you take that money?" she asked, with disbelief in her eyes.

"That's not what happened. It's not like that," I replied.

"Well, I don't want you working with me anymore," she declared.

"Okay," I said. "One day you'll know why I did this, one day you'll know the truth."

And I left. I decided to remain quiet and sacrifice my job and my friendship for our safety. I knew that if I told her the truth, she would've gone straight to social media to cuss them all out, and that would only put her life and my own in jeopardy. That's why I decided to take the hit and say nothing. She later came back at me with all she had, making incredibly harsh statements in the media about how I had stolen money from her and filing a lawsuit against me, but at least we were both alive to tell the story.

When Gabo finally filled me in on his side of the story, bringing evidence to back his claims, everything began to make more sense. The payout difference Jen saw in those invoices was the

Jenni giving it her all at a rehearsal.

Jenni and Gabo at a soundcheck before a performance.

Jenni and Edward James Olmos on the set of *Filly Brown*.

Jenni and Esteban.

Jenni getting done up by Jacob Yebale on the tour bus.

Jenni on set of *Filly Brown*.

Jenni at a photo shoot for NUVO with her Rolls Royce.

Jenni's star at Polytech High School.

Jenni with her granddaughter Jaylah and her makeup artist Jacob.

Jenni with a J-Unit fan sign.

Jenni visiting a patient at Children's Hospital Los Angeles, always ready to share her love and give back to her community and those in need.

Jenni at her "Basta ya" video shoot.

Jenni wearing her iconic fedora.

Mikey, Chiquis, Juan Rivera, Jenicka, and Jacqie next to Jenni's tour bus.

Miami nights—Pete, Zulema, Jenni, and Esteban.

Pete and Chiquis.

exact amount that had been paid as a kickback. And Gabo was all business—he knew that paying that kickback would allow them to continue working in these venues, so they were better off accepting the rules of the game and playing along than pissing these people off. On the flipside, knowing Jen, if he had told her they had to pay the cartels in order to be able to play, she would've had a hissy fit on social media, talking shit about all of them, because that's who she was. And if you look back, that's exactly what she did, but the one to take the hit was Gabo, not the cartels. He took the fall and said nothing.

Yeah, on paper, it absolutely looked like he was skimming money from the top, but now I know that wasn't the case, and now I finally get it. I understand his point of view because I knew Jen's attitude and her quick-fire reactions, and I also know that you do not mess with these people. And when all hell broke loose between Jen and Gabo, he still remained quiet, making no statements to the media, and simply keeping to himself in order to protect his life and hers too. It was the price to pay for her success in Mexico. It was something all artists had to deal with whether they knew it or not.

If you ask Gabo now, he says that in hindsight, he would have totally done things differently. Jen was like a sister to him, so he not only lost his job and reputation, he also lost one of his closest friends. In that year apart, she also missed him terribly, often reminiscing and saying, "If Gabo was here, this wouldn't be happening," when things went wrong on the road or at concerts. By not having him by her side, she was able to appreciate him even more. She noticed all that he had contributed to her career and, more than anything, she realized how much she missed her friend, her brother, her business confidant … loss number one.

Elena Jimenez

Next up was her best friend, another unforeseen disappointment and betrayal that pained Jen to the core. Jen had met Elena Jimenez two years earlier, around 2010. She was a jewelry maker and big Jenni fan, who was married to a nice, sophisticated, older woman and seemed to have a solid family life. Elena, always at Jen's beck and call, quickly earned Jen's trust and was able to access her inner circle, soon becoming one of Jen's best friends. Jen would often go to their home for dinners and allow them to babysit Johnny when she had things to do.

However, shortly after Jen's marriage to Esteban, Elena informed us that she was getting a divorce. True to Jen's essence, she was there for Elena during this tough time, having gone through divorces herself and knowing fully well how hard those life changes can be, and she also kept in touch with Sulema, whom she also considered a friend. It was during this time when some red flags popped up but went unnoticed. Sulema opened up and told Jen some stories about Elena, warning her that she wasn't all that everyone thought she was. But Jen didn't pay much mind to this, brushing it off as divorce banter. Meanwhile, Elena began to brag about all the women in business whom she had conquered, but we'd just laugh it off as fun *chismes*.

Elena eventually also became part of our team, traveling with us and attending awards, where she also catered to many other clients who wore her jewelry.

As a newly minted member of our work family, it only seemed right to include her in the big upcoming family vacation. We were in the middle of taping season two of *I Love Jenni*, which included a family trip to Hawaii, and Jen thought it would be great if Elena came along too—not only was she Jen's new best friend, but it was at her birthday party that Esteban and Jen had reconciled after their first big breakup, and now they were happily married—or so we thought—so it was a done deal. Off they went to Hawaii with the production crew in tow on their fun-filled family vacation.

After they returned, it was life as usual until Elena brought around a new girlfriend, Alejandra. I never got the clearest vibe from Alejandra, but shrugged it off; however, Chiquis didn't like her one bit. We all thought it was Chiquis being protective of her beloved inner circle, but we'd soon be proved quite wrong. The veil began to drop at Jacqie's wedding in September 2012. Elena and Alejandra were visibly upset that day. Chiquis and Elena had been whispering to each other a lot, and Alejandra looked downright pissed, but we all shrugged it off as we tried to remain focused on Jacqie's big life event.

A few days later, while Jenni was out at the movies with Esteban and her younger kids, she got an urgent call from Alejandra. This was odd, as Jen had never established any sort of bond with Alejandra. Puzzled, she answered and heard Alejandra say, "There's something I need to talk to you about." Jen was about to brush her off, but Alejandra begged and begged until Jen agreed to meet her that night. She told Esteban an unexpected meeting had come up and asked him to take the kids home, and she went off to find out what all the big fuss was about with Alejandra.

"I don't know if you know," Alejandra began, once they were face to face, "but Elena is having an affair with your daughter."

I can only imagine Jen thinking, *Holy shit!*

Alejandra produced a cell phone, claiming it was Elena's, and pulled up some photos. She slid the phone across the table to Jenni, and sure enough, there were several photos of Chiquis in a bathing suit and some other sexy shots of her daughter. Jen immediately recognized the setting: Hawaii. As Jen's heart sunk, Alejandra confessed that seeing Elena and Chiquis whispering and chatting at Jacqie's wedding gave her a funny feeling. It made her jealous. She had a hunch that something was going on between them and wanted to get to the bottom of it. So, a few nights later, as Elena was fast asleep, Alejandra grabbed her phone and flipped through the photos, stumbling upon Chiquis's swimsuit shots. Then she checked her messages and found an exchange between the two that, although not too risqué, sent her into a fit of jealousy that culminated with the phone call to Jenni.

"I'm gonna leave her," Alejandra said. "I can't do this." And that's exactly what she did. After her meeting with Jen, she ended things with Elena and moved back to Mexico.

Meanwhile, Jen was left with this bombshell and Elena's phone in hand. As she stared at those photos, she kept thinking that this was someone she had considered one of her best friends, someone she had brought into the fold as one of her own, someone she had entrusted with her family. She was completely floored and drove home livid.

The very next day Jenni called a meeting between Elena, herself, and me at Jerry's Deli down the street from her home. I had no idea what was going on and had driven over there assuming that Jen wanted to open up some more about her marital problems with Esteban, as she had done the last time we met at that same deli. However, when I strolled in with Elena, I knew something was up. As we approached Jen, who was standing there in her red and black Jordan tracksuit, she stared in our direction with teary and enraged eyes. We snagged a booth, sat down, and glanced at one another as an ominous silence hovered over us like daggers. Jen was trying to keep it together, struggling to figure out how to best approach the situation, but she couldn't hold it in any longer and let loose on Elena with every ounce of her accumulated rage.

"How could you? How could you screw around with my daughter?"

Elena sat with a dumbfounded look on her face, as if the wind had been knocked right out of her lungs, while I just sat there flabbergasted at the new drama unfolding before my eyes.

"I know all about it," Jen said, furious. "Alejandra showed me pictures and messages on your phone—so don't deny it."

"I screwed up," muttered Elena, blind-sided, with no chance of denial. "It only happened once. It was a long time ago."

By "it" Elena was referring to an alleged interaction a while back where Chiquis had gone over to Elena's home for dinner, they'd had one drink too many, and ended the night with a kiss. At least that's the story Elena told Jen.

"It only happened once?! A long time ago? Bitch, I've only known you for two years," screamed Jen in disbelief. Then she reached into her hoodie's pocket and hurled a fistful of Elena's jewelry across the table. "I don't need anything from you. You're a disgusting person and I want nothing to do with you. I have been down this road before and it hurts, but I'll get through this as I always do," she stated adamantly, then quickly glanced at her coffee cup, looked at me, and added, "Pete, you got this?"

I nodded and she stood up and left without so much as looking at Elena again. All I could think as I stared at the jewelry and at Elena was *What the hell just happened!?* Now it was my turn to gather myself. It was clear that Jen had felt wronged, and I always had her back, so I looked at Elena and, as she stared back at me like the proverbial deer in the headlights, I said, "How could you do that? She trusted you."

"It was nothing. It happened a long time ago," she stammered again.

"Elena—you screwed up," I stated as I got up, left $5 on the table, and walked out.

Meanwhile, Jen had driven back home and immediately confronted Chiquis, but she denied it all, accusing Jen of acting nuts. "Why did you take Pete and not me?!" Chiquis demanded to know. "I'm your daughter, not him." Her outbursts were meaningless to Jen, who already had Elena's confession, so then Chiquis called me. "You don't believe her, do you?!" she asked.

"I don't know what to believe, Chiquis. Either way, I think it's inappropriate." What was crystal clear was that Elena Jimenez, Jen's best friend and confidant, had been kicked out of the inner circle for good: loss number two.

Esteban Loaiza

As if losing Elena wasn't enough, Jen was in for an even bigger surprise that year, one that would signify the final nail in the coffin of her marriage with Esteban, and the most crushing blow of her life.

It was September 2012, and Jen was working on the buildout of her soon-to-be dream-come-true boutique. Julie, her assistant, texted Jen while driving to her house, letting her know the guy who was installing the cameras at the boutique needed a deposit in order to start his work. Once Julie had arrived, she walked into Jen's bedroom, while Jen went to her safe to grab the cash, since she'd just run out of checks. However, when Jen came back, instead of cash, she just had a completely baffled look on her face.

"Jules, ask him if he can start with two thousand dollars," she said quietly, brows furrowed in a state of utter confusion.

"I'm sure he can, but why can't we do the full deposit? What's wrong?" asked Julie.

"I don't have any money," she said.

"What do you mean?" asked Julie, equally confused, as she had recently helped her put away some cash in the safe and other spots around the room.

"I have four thousand dollars, and I wanted to give my mom money, but I have no money to give. Take half and see what you can do. I'm going to my mom's."

Jen kept replaying the last few months over and over again in her mind the rest of the day. There were only three people who knew the combination to Jen's safe: Jen, Julie, and Jen's cousin, Tere, her home office assistant. In fact, she'd had the combination changed when Chiquis moved out earlier that year, so not even Chiquis had access to her savings. Additionally, a couple of months earlier, in July 2012, sometime around her birthday, Jen and I had spent four hours counting all her earnings from her tours, so she and I both knew that two months earlier there had been well over $900,000 in that safe. Where did all that loot go between July and September? Something was crazy wrong. Jen didn't want to think it was Julie, but she also didn't know what to think. Then she started suspecting Esteban. The night before, she had finally asked him for some space, having been feeling that their marriage had been off kilter for a while. So he went to his mother's and took a small piece of luggage with him. She'd assumed it held his belongings, but now she wasn't so sure.

The following morning, when Julie arrived at the house, Jen asked her to go up to Esteban's man cave and look around.

"Look for what?" Julie asked.

"I don't know, but I have a feeling you will find something," Jen said, now on a mission to get to the bottom of the mysterious disappearance of her cash.

Julie agreed, went upstairs, and turned the man cave upside down, coming across endless binders filled with Esteban's account statements. As she flipped through them, she quickly noticed that he had blown through all his money. There were also IRS letters and other receipts. She was shuffling through everything when she noticed an envelope hiding behind an old shoe box. When she grabbed it she immediately saw the safe's combination scribbled down in Esteban's handwriting, with exact instructions, "Number, turn left three times, number, turn right." She brought this piece of paper to Jen, who simply said, "Dumbass couldn't just write the numbers, he had to write the damn instructions too."

That's when they reached out to me, and I in turn contacted our lawyer, Anthony, and filled him in on what was going on. After hearing all the details, Anthony decided to send someone to fingerprint the safe. The more evidence we could gather, the better. When the lady arrived at Jen's house, they mentioned the envelope, but in order to fingerprint it, it would have to go through a specific chemical that would inevitably destroy the paper, so we all decided against that. Instead, Julie went out and bought a smaller safe, put the envelope in a Ziploc bag, and Jen stored it in the new safe, feeling that her old one had now been completely compromised.

There was only one thing left to do: review the surveillance footage. Jen had surveillance cameras set up throughout the house, so she decided to grab the video and start reviewing about a week back, unaware that what she was about to see would wreck her heart. As she glanced through the footage, one specific moment caught her attention, so she paused, rewound, and carefully observed the image sequence. The light in her bedroom bathroom was on, and she saw two people going into her huge walk-in closet. The closet lights were off, so it was impossible to see exactly what happened in there, but it was clear that the two people walked out of the closet thirty-nine minutes later. What blew Jen's mind was that the two people leaving the room, the two people who had just spent thirty-nine minutes in her closet, in the dark, were none other than Chiquis and Esteban. Her heart stopped. The next shot was one of Chiquis leaving the room, crossing the hallway, walking down the stairs and out the front door. Shortly after, Esteban can be seen going into the bathroom. If that bathroom light hadn't been on, Jen would've never noticed this strange and agonizing sequence of events.

As if all this weren't enough, Jen noticed that this little stint in the closet had gone down on the same night Jen was listening to Alejandra as she spilled the beans on the whole Elena and Chiquis affair. Then, in addition to this troublesome discovery, she also found footage of Esteban going into her safe, taking bricks of cash, and stuffing them into a black Prada bag. Suddenly tangled in a web of lies and deception, she wasn't sure what to tackle first. She paused and then called me.

"I'm going to file for divorce. The minute I have the paperwork we'll drive to San Diego, where his family lives. Will you serve him his papers?" she asked.

"Absolutely," I said, ready to do whatever was necessary to help my sister out.

A woman of action, Jen filed for divorce on October 1, and we drove down to serve him on October 2. It was his mother's birthday, so she had already previously arranged this visit, but Esteban had no idea what was about to hit him. Clueless, he simply thought Jen was driving down to have dinner with him and help celebrate his mom's day. Meanwhile, Jen had also asked her Mexican lawyer, Mario Macías, to fly to San Diego, so he could be there with us when it all went down, and he did.

I drove on our way over there while Jen quietly sat by my side in the passenger's seat, focused on the message she was drafting. At one point, I interrupted her, as I felt the urge to tell her something. Chiquis and Jen had been on the outs for a while, so I knew what I was about to say could cost me, but I wanted to be frank with her.

"I want you to know that I considered working with Chiquis."

She stopped what she was doing, rested her back against the car door, stared at me, and said, "Okay …"

"I met with her at my house and also met with Angel," I continued. Angel was Chiquis's boyfriend at the time. I explained that I thought Chiquis definitely had potential and could do something, but in the end, I couldn't bring myself to leave my friend for her daughter.

Jen's eyes softened as she smiled and said, "I know you, and I knew you wouldn't leave me."

I didn't want to cause her any more pain, but I also didn't want to take any part in the web of lies and deception that surrounded her. She was my sister by choice and I always wanted to do right by her.

After clearing the air, we picked up Mario, and, as we drove the last stretch to Esteban's house, Jen turned her attention back to her phone. She was furiously drafting an e-mail to Esteban and Chiquis, with one subject line: "You should have turned the lights off." She took the time to detail everything she saw on the tape, revised it three times, and read it out loud to us in the car. Those thirty-nine minutes killed my friend. Those were the thirty-nine minutes that managed to pulverize her world and her heart.

As we neared Esteban's house, Jen laid out the plan. "I'll go into his house and when I'm ready, I'll text you and Mario, and then you guys ring the doorbell."

Jen got out of the car, walked up to the main entrance, and rang the doorbell and his parents let her in. Esteban was out running an errand, so Jen excused herself, pretending she needed to use the bathroom, but as she headed down the hallway, she snuck into Esteban's room and started grabbing all the jewelry she could get her hands on. "The asshole stole from me? Well, Imma steal from his ass." No way was he going to get away with it all without suffering the wrath of Jenni. Meanwhile, Mario and I noticed Esteban's Lamborghini pulling around the corner, so we got ready, knowing all hell was about to break loose.

A few minutes after he stepped into his house, we got the text from Jen to make our move. When the door opened, Jen let Esteban have it. "I know everything, you piece of shit." He stared back at her in a daze, not knowing exactly what she was talking about. Then Jen turned and addressed his family, given that they had been so adamant about her signing a prenup. "Did you know that your prince of a son has been stealing money from me?" she asked his mom. And then she proceeded to tell them everything, from the footage of him stealing, to the paper with the combination in his writing, and the mysterious time he spent with her daughter in the closet. She wanted to make sure they knew what their freeloading son had been up to those past few months; she wanted them to feel ashamed for having raised someone like him in this world.

Esteban's only response to Jen's outrage was, "I got my own money." Then, Jen pulled out her wedding photo and handed it to Esteban's mom. "Here—all yours. So you can remember." Meanwhile, I tried to serve him the divorce papers, but he didn't want to take them from me. He followed Jen outside and threw the photo at us, aggression pouring out of his pores, as if he were on the brink of hitting her. His mom followed him outside, screaming and calling Jen names. "¡Puta! Our son has no reason to steal from anyone! We raised a good son!"

Then I turned to Esteban and said, "Let it go," trying to keep him at bay. "It's over." And with that, I gave him the papers and we left. Once we were in the car, Jen showed us she had also made out with his iPad, which now she had good reason to believe was likely paid for with her own money. As she was showing it to us, we noticed it was still connected to his iPhone and, thanks to the synergy of Apple products, we saw Esteban was texting Chiquis. "Delete my messages. Your mom is on to us," read his text.

That was it, that was the final straw that broke this camel's back. Jen went absolutely ape-shit. She opened the e-mail she'd been drafting on the drive down and hit send with zero qualms and no remorse. Moments later our phones started blowing up. I began getting calls from Angel, Juan, Chiquis, and Esteban. Nonstop. Everyone wanted to tell me Jenni was crazy, but no one wanted to believe or even be sympathetic to her. In the two hours it took us to get home, the fire had been ignited and lines were drawn in the sand. The family was divided and so was the team. Loss number three was disappointing and embittering, but loss number four was the final blow.

Chapter 11

Paloma Negra

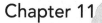

jennirivera
@jennirivera

if I am an evil mother I will pay for it...if not...I will be rewarded. Period. For now, all I want is to move on...continue the journey and continue to count my blessings. Existen muchas cosas y personas en mi vida, en estos momentos, por los cuales tengo que estar feliz y plena. Enough is enough...I must move on. Gracias, y buenas noches.

2012-11-15

osing a man wasn't a big deal for Jen, but losing a daughter was unthinkable. The pain she felt by Chiquis's betrayal was seeded with profound and unquestionable love. In order to understand the depths of this agony, you must first understand their deep-seated bond.

Chiquis was so much more than Jen's first-born. She was her beloved daughter, her best friend, and her sergeant at home.

Since Jen was only sixteen when she had her, their relationship didn't follow the traditional mother and daughter roles. They'd been in the trenches together, dealing with abuse and poverty, learning from their mistakes, celebrating each success, and building a bond based on trust and transparency. So when Jen decided to give her musical career a real shot, when she decided to take herself seriously as an artist, when she realized there was a business opportunity within arm's reach for her to do what she loved and make a living out of it, she dove in head first, while Chiquis held down the fort at home. By this time, it wasn't just the two of them. Jen already had another four children in tow, so Chiquis's support was invaluable.

While Jen was out on tour, building her career and providing for her family, Chiquis was at home tending to her siblings' needs. Unknowingly, Jen had slowly taken on the dad's role in the family, working long hours to put food on the table, and Chiquis naturally gravitated to the mom's role, taking care of the kids and managing the money at home. Mind you, we're not talking about a grown woman here, we're talking about a young girl taking on these adult responsibilities to lend a helping hand to her hard-working mom. While Jen went off to work, Chiquis sacrificed going to college to support her family. Chiquis was actually the one who allowed Jen to become the star everyone knows and loves. Jen couldn't have done it without her.

Not only did Chiquis hold down the fort at home, she also served as her mom's stylist, driving downtown to buy Jen's costume jewelry and clothing, making sure to pick out the most figure-flattering dresses for her mom. And Jen trusted and relied on her blindly. Chiquis was without a doubt her right hand for many years and she knew her mom inside and out. So much so that when I joined Jen's team, if I had a question and Jen wasn't available to answer it, I'd turn to Chiquis, who was always there, sharp and bubbly, ready to provide the necessary information for all of us to get the job done.

Chiquis was Jen's everything. Now, this doesn't mean their relationship was not without its own strains. One time, yearning for her independence like any normal teenager, Chiquis dropped everything and ran away from home. She sought shelter with her Tío Lupillo, a decision that was a direct jab at Jen. It almost felt intentional because Chiquis knew all too well how difficult it was for Jen to deal with Lupillo's lack of support for her career, so that move definitely hurt her. To Chiquis's credit, in seeking her independence and running away, she did try to break away from her family by getting a job at the mall; however, Lupillo ended up putting her up at one of his apartments and made sure she was cared for financially. Jen was seething inside. It was difficult to watch her partner in crime cross that line and, out of all people, go to Lupillo for help. Hoping to ease her pain, I often reminded Jen that he was still her uncle, and it was better she reached out to him than a stranger off the street, but I'm not sure how much that helped her deal with this situation.

Nevertheless, their bond was so strong that two months later, mother and daughter reconciled and, although Jen had made a few changes and had hired a personal assistant, Chiquis stepped right back into her role as house manager, caregiver, daughter, sister, and princess. No matter what they went through, no matter the ups and downs, the fights, the rebellions, Jen absolutely adored her children. She considered her sons princes and her daughters princesses, and often called them prince and princess endearingly.

Jen wanted nothing more than for her kids to be happy and successful in life. She had learned to give one hundred percent to everything she did, and she expected nothing less from her children. Regardless of whether they wished to be dishwashers, gardeners, nurses, artists, or astronauts, all Jen cared about was making sure that they knew how to commit to reach their goals, often reminding them, "Whatever you choose to do, do your best at it and give it your all." Even though she had become the family's sole provider, Jen took her role as a mother very seriously. She may not have been present for some of their day-to-day events, but she always made sure to make time for them when she was home, encouraging them to have an honest and open relationship with her. And they knew that even though she had to be on the road to provide for them, she always had their backs.

Jen was a mama bear in all her glory and was ready to fight tooth and nail for her children no matter the circumstances. That's why I believe having failed to protect Chiquis from her ex-husband's abuse made her feel like she had failed her daughter in the worst possible way, and it filled her life with guilt, a guilt that sometimes led her to overcompensate while raising her, becoming somewhat of an enabler when the going got tough at home. I experienced firsthand the many difficult times Chiquis had to face throughout her early life, her mother's second divorce, her father's trial, her mom's sex tape, and countless other highs and lows in Jen's roller coaster of a life. Chiquis proved to be a resilient young lady, much like her mother, but she was also struggling to find herself in a family filled with big characters, a quest she clearly embarked on once their reality show was released.

It was during the start of *I Love Jenni* that we first noticed major changes in Chiquis's behavior. With the boyfriends and the partying and the excessive shopping, she was suddenly becoming another one of those Hollywood brats, which went against every fiber of Jen's being. Needless to say, that's when this mother-daughter relationship began hitting bigger hurdles. The very first crackles of their estrangement really happened in the fall of 2011 when Jen decided it was time to start teaching her daughter the importance of fiscal responsibility.

Until then Chiquis worked at Jen's office, running all the admin related to Jen's bustling career. In this capacity Chiquis controlled her mama's accounts, gathering Jen's earnings and paying all the bills. Jen was never a fan of using credit cards, but every now and again, like everyone else, she had to. On one of those occasions her card was denied. Being Jenni Rivera, this was a complete embarrassment. She called Chiquis right away, inquiring about the situation.

"Hey, Princess, what's going on with the card?" Jen asked.

"Oh, they must have blocked it, Mom," said Chiquis, dodging the issue.

However, when Jen's cards began getting denied with more frequency, it became clear she needed to take matters into her own hands. She knew it was time to do a little digging. What she found was unsettling: charges for trips to Las Vegas with bottle service and bills racking up $3,500 a night, plane tickets, clothes, and all types of lavish living that were above and beyond anything Jen herself would entertain. *What the hell*, thought Jen. *Did I raise a Kardashian?* Jen flipped. We're talking about a woman who moved mountains to get her family off the ground and give them a better chance at life, someone who worked tirelessly for every single penny she earned. Jen knew the value of a dollar all too well. Once she started doing well, when she wanted something, yeah, she got it, but she didn't go out and blow her money for the hell of it. She wasn't cheap, but life had taught her to be frugal, so Chiquis's behavior had gone too far in her book. Jen realized the time had come to stop enabling her daughter and start teaching her about accountability.

"I think you have a problem," Jen told her daughter point-blank on the phone one day. "You don't need all this stuff. We have plenty."

Chiquis had no way out. She knew she had dug herself in too deep. Her lifestyle had finally caught up with her. She apologized and admitted to her mom that she had a problem with money.

"If that's true, I think the best thing is for you to earn some independence by learning responsibility," Jen said.

And with that, Jen decided that the time had come for Chiquis to move out of the house and live on her own. Jen figured that if Chiquis went out and earned her own money and paid her own bills, she'd eventually learn how to better manage her own finances and truly understand the value of each dime in her pocket. At the time we were also shooting *Chiquis in Control*, a spin-off of our *I Love Jenni* series. Jen thought we should back out of production as part of this new effort to really educate Chiquis on the subject of autonomy; however, knowing it was Chiquis's first time out in the real world, Jen gave her $100,000 to help her embark on this new journey. Meanwhile, Chiquis also received another $100,000 from the production company, so she was well-armed to get her series up and running with this financial boost and finally have the independent life she had so yearned for when she ran away from home a few years earlier.

It all seemed like a fantastic starting point. Chiquis was well-poised to hit the ground running, but her show flopped.

The first two episodes were flat and stale, so the network called a meeting to let us know they couldn't air it as is. Their one condition to move forward was if Jen and the kids were more involved. Jen agreed to support the show and her daughter, and stepped in with cameos by her and her children. However, this was a rude awakening for Chiquis. She believed she'd be able to follow her mother's lead, but without her mother's support, it was a no-go. And so began a burgeoning tension between them that would eventually implode causing irreparable damages to their lifelong bond.

Those were trying times, but they helped Jen grow as a mother in patience, love, and kindness, doing all she could to push her daughter in the right direction in hopes that she would find her way, until their relationship hit yet another hurdle: Angel del Villar. When Chiquis started dating Angel, president and owner of Del Records, Jen was leery of him from the get-go. He had a reputation that Jen didn't like and most definitely didn't want that for her daughter, but there wasn't much she could do. After all, she was the one who had suggested Chiquis become independent and try her hand at making her own decisions. So there she was, doing what her mama said; only instead of finding her own way, she had found Angel.

Once the summer of 2012 came around, the relationship between Angel and Chiquis heated up, and they were clearly an official item. Jen still didn't approve, and Angel knew this, so he decided to throw Chiquis a party at his house just for her family. I wasn't planning on attending, but Jen called and invited me to come along, so I said yes. I knew she had her doubts about this guy and wanted help deciphering him. I honestly thought that Angel was finally trying to extend an olive branch to Jen. There was booze, music, and dancing, and everyone seemed to be having a good time. Then Angel approached Jen and asked to speak with her privately. Once again, he seemed sincere in his gentlemanly approach.

"I love your daughter," he said, "and I want to be with her."

"What do you really want?" she asked. Jenni wasn't having it. She didn't buy the whole chivalrous act because she just couldn't get around the fact that he was still married to another woman. Yes, he was married, and that was not only completely unacceptable to her, it also proved that he couldn't possibly be as serious about Chiquis as he stated. Suffice to say, that party did nothing to win Jen over, but Angel stayed the course and stuck by Chiquis, despite being married. He even helped her finance her new business venture, a blow-dry salon. When she fell short for little things like the electric sign, Angel swooped in to save the day. He also took over Jen's role as Chiquis's chief sponsor and provider of luxuries. It went against everything Jen was hoping to teach her daughter by asking her to move out of the house, but again, there was nothing she could do at this point but just sit back and watch it all unfold before her eyes.

Then came Jacqie's wedding in September 2012. You already know about the whole Elena debacle that happened a few days after this big event, but something else had gone down earlier, something that didn't just anger Jen—it actually worried and frightened her. A few days prior to the wedding, Jen's brother, Gustavo, received a private message through Facebook from a woman who claimed to be Angel's wife. In it she told Chiquis to leave her husband alone. She explained that they had children and homes together and that, although she'd been in Mexico attending family business, she knew what Angel had been up to.

Shocked, Gustavo immediately contacted Jen and showed her the message. She then filled me in on what was going on. As if that weren't enough, we also had reason to believe Angel's scorned wife had ties to important people in Mexico, the type you don't want to mess with, so now what? As always, the show must go on.

Jacqie's big day arrived, and as I got dressed, it already felt like a disaster in the making. This was a big day for Jen. Her second daughter was getting married, the first one of her children to get hitched. It should've been a glorious moment, but it was fraught with palpable tension. On one hand, Jen had to deal with some wedding drama: Jacqie's groom had previously dated Jen's sister Rosie—a fact that still unsettled certain members of the Rivera family on the supposedly blissful day, like Juan who, much to Jen's disappointment, was unable to hide his long face throughout the ceremony. On the other hand, I could tell that even though Jen was doing all she could to be present and happy for her princess on this wonderful occasion, her mind kept wandering back to that message. The clash with Chiquis had stopped being only about a mother's concern for her daughter. Now it was also about pissing off the wrong family, the kind of family that would have zero qualms dealing with your ass, which only reinforced Jen's opinion about her daughter's love interest.

After much thought, Jen decided to confront the situation head on, as always. She talked to Chiquis and told her what was going on, making her feelings about Angel crystal clear, but Chiquis wouldn't have it. Rather than paying attention to what

Jen was telling her, she immediately accused her mom of being a hypocrite for accepting Jacqie's husband, knowing he'd also once dated Rosie, and not accepting Angel in the same way. She wasn't able to see how different these situations were. Blinded by love, she couldn't see that she was playing with fire, and all Jen was hoping to do was stop her from getting seriously burned.

As if all this drama weren't enough, shortly after Jacqie's wedding, in a matter of weeks, Jen found out about Elena's dalliances with Chiquis, losing her best friend in the process, and then came across that heart-wrenching surveillance footage, which culminated in her filing for divorce and cutting ties with her daughter for good. As was customary with the Riveras when the shit hit the fan, Jen called a family meeting to prep them for the upcoming divorce and also talk about the whole Chiquis situation. Here's the clincher: one might think the footage would have been enough to prove Chiquis's betrayal, but since the video didn't show exactly what happened between Esteban and Chiquis in that closet, even though Jen deemed it radically inappropriate, the family had their doubts regarding Jen's harsh accusations. Meanwhile, Chiquis never really gave Jen a clear explanation justifying why she had been in that closet with Esteban. She simply denied it, claiming Jen was out of her mind.

So when Jen walked into that family meeting and gave them the play by play, she suddenly found she had little to no support, until the person she least expected took the stand and defended her like no other. She thought Juan would be the one to take her side, having always been her *consentido*, the one she'd babied and taken on tour and coddled. But while Juan sat at the table quietly, the one who first jumped up and spoke was none other than Lupillo. Jen loved her brother Lupillo dearly. They had always loved each other, but there was no denying that the past decade had been fraught with competition and sibling rivalry. Their careers had taken a toll on their relationship, so seeing Lupillo speak up for her took her completely by surprise. "Look, sis, right or wrong, you're my sister, and it's my obligation to support my sister not my niece. If you're wrong, then we're going to be wrong together, but I'm supporting you."

Jen and Chiquis had had other falling outs, but this was the first time her brother came forward and made her feel his full support—it was also the first time she'd felt his full support in one of the crucial moments of her life. She was moved beyond words. After the meeting, as Jen drove home, she called me to share this unbelievable moment, and I rejoiced with her. Every cloud has a silver lining, and this time around the silver lining was finally being able to bury the hatchet with her brother Lupillo. A spark of joy amid the darkest of days.

Jen's issues with Chiquis erupted into total estrangement and tore her apart. She couldn't wrap her mind around what the hell her daughter had been doing in that closet with her husband. Filled with doubts and insecurities, having a gut feeling, but not knowing what to think, Jen's pain worsened, but no matter how heart-wrenching this situation had become, she wasn't about to go out and bash her daughter in public, in the media, because in the end, she loved her. She was a reflection of herself. Even through the pain, she wanted to protect her, but Jen and Chiquis's problems were still far from over.

In early November 2012, just about a month before the fatal crash in Mexico, Jen was invited to a music award show in L.A., and she'd decided to attend. As was usual with her, no matter what drama she was dealing with at home, she always managed to keep it together for her career. I hadn't planned on being there with her until I got a worried call from Julie, her assistant. She told me Angel was roaming the area, and it looked like he had been drinking. I dropped everything, got in my car, and sped over there as fast as possible, knowing this couldn't amount to any good. Meanwhile, Jen had a camera crew with her getting footage for *I Love Jenni*, and as they were making their way down one of the narrow hallways backstage toward her dressing room, Angel aggressively bumped into one of our cameramen with a no-one-gets-in-my-way attitude, shoving his way down the corridor like a high school bully. Jen hadn't noticed any of it until she saw the look on my face when I walked into her dressing room. She immediately realized that something was off. As she continued to sign autographs and snap pics with fans, she asked me, "What's going on?"

"We need to get out of here," I said. "Let's avoid any drama with Angel." I explained to her that he was there and seemed to be sniffing around for trouble. So I arranged for a car to meet her out front, where she got in with her makeup and hair stylists as I walked over to my own vehicle, which I'd valet parked. As Jen's car pulled away, she noticed a fan trying to say hi. Always ready to please her fans, grateful for their support, she rolled down her window to greet her, but not until that split second did she realize that standing next to this woman was Angel, who began talking shit and insulting her, calling her awful names right there on the street, in front of everyone, a moment that was captured on video and went viral years ago. Not one to stand down, Jen got out of the car like a true gangster and beelined over to him, only to be met by the barricade of security guards surrounding him, but that didn't stop her. I ran over to her, made my way through the crowd, picked her up and brought her back to the car, but before getting back in, she stood on the door frame and got her two cents in there for everyone to see.

"If you wanna talk, call me. When I pass by don't talk to me, *porque si tienes algo que decir*, you say it in my damn face!".

Angel narrowed his eyes and replied, "Yeah, we'll see," with a smirk on his face that downright gave me the chills, but I had no time to process this because the crowds began to swarm around us, so I put Jen in the car and shut the door. As they zoomed off, I suddenly noticed she was being followed by a black van. I ran over to my car, drove out, and quickly realized I was being followed too. What the hell! We were near the Gibson Theater with shitty cell phone reception, so I couldn't get through to Jen immediately. When I finally was able to connect, I said as calmly as possible, "Don't go home. Stay on the freeway. You're being followed." In a panic, Jen turned around and replied, "I see him, I see him!" Now it began to settle in: we were officially in danger. However, after driving a while longer, we managed to lose both vans. All I could think was that they were likely trying to send us a message to scare us. In any case, that night I went to Jen's house and gave her a gun. I also set up a security guard on the street outside her house. I didn't mention this last bit to her because I knew she wouldn't agree, but I didn't want us taking any chances–I wanted to make sure she was safe.

What followed was a social media barrage attacking Chiquis. "That's your boyfriend? That's the guy you're fighting for? That's the man that you say loves you? That disrespects your mother?" Jen was pissed, and scared, and worried, but there wasn't much else she could do.

Meanwhile, the next morning I decided to take matters into my own hands. I couldn't just sit around and wait, so I drove to Angel's office. I felt we needed to hash out what had happened the night before. He wasn't there, so I left a message and got a call back from him later.

"Pete, it's not personal. I have nothing personal with *you*—it's with *her*."

We hung up and as I was driving home, while I was talking to Jen on my Bluetooth, I suddenly got rear-ended on the freeway. Shocked, I yelled out, "I got hit!" Jen couldn't see what was going on, so she immediately assumed that what she heard on the other side of the line was gunfire, rather than my car being totaled. She freaked out. "Where are you?! Where are you?!" she screamed at the top of her lungs. I will never forget the care and concern in her voice that day as she was forced to entertain life without me. The irony of it all haunts me to this day.

Everything just spiraled downward from there. It was almost Thanksgiving. Jen was busy filming *La Voz* in Mexico, but managed to get a few days off for the holiday, which we were filming for her reality show. We were also working on a show about her brother, Juan, her lifelong *consentido*, but since the drama with Chiquis, the family was divided, and Juan, whom I guess believed Chiquis, didn't want much to do with Jen anymore. Feeling alienated and hurt, Jen no longer knew where to turn.

We had many talks around that time, especially late at night when she couldn't sleep. Jen kept going back to her surveillance footage, wondering what her daughter and husband were doing in that closet. Those foggy images haunted her till the day she died. I honestly don't think it was an affair. If anything, it's possible they were accomplices after some of her money. Why do I think that? It turned out Esteban was broke and had a major IRS lien; meanwhile, Chiquis wasn't living at home, had money issues, and didn't have the means to keep up with her Hollywood lifestyle. Both seemed to have motives, but we will never know for sure. Only Esteban, Chiquis, and God know what happened that night in the closet. All I know is that it was the straw that broke the camel's back in Jen's world.

About a week after Thanksgiving, my father passed away, and that's when we had our last heart-to-heart talk in the hospital parking lot, the one where I was able to see the weight of her life and pain through her sorrowful brown eyes, the one where I realized my dear friend was truly broken and lost. From where I was standing, the last year of Jen's life read like a game of emotional Rubik's Cube. Things kept coming at her with that when-it-rains-it-pours ferocity, and just when one thing seemed to be handled, the next one would start to unfurl. Her world at home was coming undone before her eyes, but her career was in full swing. And no matter what was going on in her personal life, Jen knew that the show had to go on. Work wasn't only a duty she had to fulfill, it was her safe haven, her shelter, a place where she felt loved and supported, a refuge where she could face her inner demons and openly let the tears stream down her face. And that's exactly what she did on December 8, 2012, in the Monterrey Arena, as she belted out "Paloma Negra," the last song she sang on this earth, dedicated to none other than her beloved Chiquis.

Watching that performance is still heart-wrenching to this day. It was so raw, so authentic, Jen at her finest, darkest, deepest hour, singing to her daughter because, despite all their disagreements and all the pain they caused each other, one thing remained intact: LOVE. A love that clearly shines through the tears rolling down Jen's cheeks as she sang, "*Pero mis ojos se mueren sin mirar tus ojos, y mi cariño con la aurora te vuelve a esperar*" ... *but my eyes will die without looking into yours, and my love with the dawn will await you again.*

Chapter 12

Lights Out

jennirivera
@jennirivera

I am going through difficult times in my life, once again. However, as has always happened, a major blessing comes after a major trial and tribulation. It never fails. Maybe thats the reason I have mastered the art of lifting myself up after a painful fall, because I look forward to the blessings that are coming. The Diva keeps her head up and smiles. Good day.

2012-10-12

" [I live in a] butterfly house, for a butterfly woman who is still going through a metamorphosis," said Jen in one of her last episodes on her reality show *I Love Jenni* in the fall of 2012. It was a Christmas episode, but Jen was far from being in the Christmas spirit. She was a wreck, devastated by the downfall of her relationship with Chiquis, but still trying to put on a happy face for her family. "How about for just one year we cancel Christmas," Jen suggests in that same episode. She couldn't fathom celebrating Christmas without her daughter. She was disappointed and profoundly hurt by everything that had happened, but she still loved and missed Chiquis terribly. No matter what trials and tribulations they faced, Jen's children were her tribe. They were far from a perfect and average family, but the bond of love they shared helped them overcome every obstacle they encountered together. And, had it not been for her fatal accident, I believe this very same bond would've eventually led to a Jen and Chiquis reconciliation. Unfortunately, time was not on their side.

As Jen walked through the valley of the shadow of death, despite the pain she carried regarding her daughter, she did experience a few sparks of happiness before her passing that filled her with hope for a better 2013, a year that would never come to be in her life, but one she had faith would be extraordinary. The first sparks came in the form of reconciliations, first with Gabo and then with Lupillo.

After firing Gabo, Jen was furious. She dismembered him in the media and followed it up by filing a law suit against him for not carrying a booking agent license. That was classic Jenni—when she was wronged, she lunged straight for the jugular. Yet, despite the defamation and case against him, Gabo remained quiet. He didn't throw her under the bus, he didn't try to get his version out there, and he didn't try to justify his actions because he knew that if he said a word, he'd put both his life and that of Jenni's at risk. So he took every hit in silence, hoping that one day the truth would come out and all would finally be out in the open.

And sure enough, as 2011 and 2012 unfolded, the truth slowly began to see the light of day. When Gabo left, Mario Macías eased his way into the team and took his place. And as he booked Jen's gigs in Mexico, he also explained that they had to pay to play. "What do you mean?" asked Jen, somewhat confused. "Gabo never gave them anything. He'd made an arrangement and didn't have to pay." To which Mario responded, "Well, I don't know how he did it because if we don't pay up, we're putting our lives at risk and we could lose it all." That's when Jen first began to realize that Gabo had been paying kickbacks in Mexico against her will. "No wonder he never told me. I'd strictly forbidden him from doing this, but now I see that it was for our safety," she said to Julie later that year. Then she started putting two and two together and began wondering if maybe that missing money in those famous invoices was actually money that had gone to pay these kickbacks. She wasn't sure, but what she did know was that the ship without Gabo at the helm in Mexico wasn't running as smoothly as it had been, and she started softening her stance against him.

Nevertheless, Gabo remained on the outs with Jen until October 2012 rolled around and he got wind of her imminent divorce. When the announcement went public, Gabo was genuinely concerned about his friend. He didn't care how bad it had gotten between them. He wasn't worried about work; he just wanted to know how his friend was doing. He'd seen her through so many ups and down in the roller coaster that was her life that he was sincerely sad to find out her "happily ever after" hadn't worked out and felt the need to reach out and let her know she was in his thoughts.

"I know how hard it must be for you and your children," said Gabo in an e-mail he drafted and sent Jen when he heard about the divorce. "I can't offer you my support because I know you won't accept it. But I can tell you that you are in my prayers, and I hope that you are soon able to overcome this new challenge that God has put in your path. You will overcome it."

Five minutes later, Jen replied, "Thanks for taking the time to write, keeping me in your thoughts and prayers. I still love you … and I miss you a lot."

Gabo's eyes filled with tears as he read her words. It was such a healing moment. Receiving that e-mail to Jen was gold. From that day forward, until the day she passed, they continued communicating. In a later e-mail, Jen wrote: "I always tell everyone how much I miss you … so many moments we shared together, the good, the bad, the successes, the failures … unforgettable experiences." And later on, she also wrote: "I'd love to be your friend … I love you … you're my brother … even more so than some of my own brothers. I hope we can get together for dinner and some drinks."

The road to reconciliation had finally been paved and they were both elated. As Gabo recalls, "On December 7, she sent me a text saying she was busy working the next few days, but that we should see each other on Wednesday, December 12, in L.A. at Gloria Trevi's concert. And I replied, 'Don't worry, I'll be there,' but she never made it."

I know she wanted Gabo back on the team. She missed him. He played a major role in her career. He witnessed her every sacrifice and was right there with her, helping her climb to the top, giving her the push she needed to keep going when the going got extra tough. I knew how much he meant to her, but I was still wary. Jen had to convince me to relax my position with him, to be more open to their reconciliation. I was a protective big brother who simply didn't want to see her in more pain than she already was, but I finally agreed to follow her lead. To make amends, the

three of us were going to meet at that Gloria Trevi concert on
December 12, 2012, the week after her concert in Monterrey.
Jen was planning on dropping the case against him and asking
him to rejoin the team in January, but that reunion never came
to pass. I take comfort in knowing that at the very least they were
able to communicate and patch things up before she died. It not
only gave Gabo a sense of peace, but I know it also filled Jen with
some hope at a time when she desperately needed it.

The other key person who made her heavy heart brim with joy
during those dark days was none other than her brother Lupillo.
When he stood up for her at their family meeting, saying he'd
remain by her side whether she was right or wrong, and lending
her the support she had always yearned to receive from him,
Jen's issues with her brother melted away. It was one of the most
endearing moments of her life that year, one that finally brought
these two siblings together, reconciled at last. So, toward the end
of November, while Jen was on a business trip in Mexico, when
she heard that her brother was playing at the Texcoco Rodeo just
outside of Mexico City, she was ecstatic when she realized she was
free that night. "Look, I wanna go see my brother's show," she said
to her team in Mexico, and they made it happen.

The beauty of it all was that Lupillo had no idea she'd be
there, so when Jen took the stage in the middle of one of his
songs, tears started streaming down Lupillo's face. Completely
taken aback and genuinely surprised, he embraced her in a long
and affectionate hug that meant more than anyone could have
imagined. "I've been waiting for this visit for seven years, and
now that I've gotten it, I'm crying like a little boy, *me vale madre*,
I cry too!" They sang together and before leaving the stage, Jen
thanked the audience, thanked her brother, and publicly said,

"Now that I needed my brother, he's been here for me, so I ask for a big round of applause for my brother!"

It was a wonderful moment for them both, a genuine and major public reconciliation, something that left Jen filled with happiness and peace, and gave Lupillo the comfort he needed to deal with her passing a few weeks later. I'm so grateful that God allowed that orchestration of healing between them before her accident. I'm also grateful that He allowed one more crucial meeting to take place right before Jen's passing, one that also sparked joy and reminded her that even though her inner circle of trust seemed to be crumbling and imploding, there were still people she loved that she could lean on, and they'd always have her back. She received this gift the night she met up with her beloved Pelón on a rooftop overlooking the City of Angels.

I found out about this get-together the next morning, a few days before the accident, when she called me at 7:00 a.m. sharp, as she usually did, and said, "Guess where I'm coming from?"

"I don't know," I said, clueless. "The gym?"

"From Ferni's."

"What do you mean you're coming from Ferni's? What's up?" I said, protectively. The last thing she needed was more drama.

"No, no, it wasn't like that," she said, calming me down. "We just had an amazing night. We got on the roof with two chairs and just talked the whole night away until the sun came up." Fernando lived on Hollywood Boulevard and from his apartment, you could see the Sunset Strip.

"You just talked all night?" I asked, incredulous.

"Yes! It was unbelievable," she replied.

They spent the night reminiscing, connecting as soul mates, as best friends. She cherished that moment like no other, especially given the circumstances, because it was plain and simple, just hanging out with an old friend who understood her. He too had been through a lot overcoming his addictions, so he got everything she'd been through and could comprehend her current trials and tribulations, no explanations needed. He got her and, ten years later, he was clean and still there by her side, sharing yet another unique night as they overlooked the city lights below and the stars above.

On December 4, 2012, just five days before the plane crash, Jen had landed another mega milestone in her career, and a ground-breaking first for Latinas in the entertainment industry: we signed a deal with ABC for Jenni's future sitcom. Yes, she was going to have her own sitcom, a la Lucille Ball or Roseanne; only this time it would also mean she'd be the first Latina to land a leading comedic role on American TV. Up until then, Latinas had been featured as part of an ensemble, such as Eva Longoria on *Desperate Housewives* or Sofia Vergara on *Modern Family*, but no Latina had ever gotten the lead role, until now. That deal not only guaranteed us a million dollars, it also fit perfectly well with another gig she'd landed earlier: A Las Vegas residency in August 2013, also another first for her as a Latina and in her music genre, which guaranteed an additional eight million dollars. That was it, that was all she needed to make her main goal in 2013 a reality.

Yes, these were groundbreaking projects, milestones, but the most important accomplishment of all would've been to stop touring for a while and make her dream of being closer to her children finally come true. Since these were both local ventures, she wouldn't have to travel far to get to work, and would finally be able to be the mom she had always wanted to be for her kids. She said it best in one of our last conversations when we were going over our goals for the upcoming year.

"I'm so looking forward to just being a mom."

"But you've been a mom all this time," I said.

"No," she replied. "I've been so busy all these years being a provider, the dad's role, that I'm finally looking forward to just being a mom, to make my kids breakfast, pick them up from school."

And I got it. Jen had been providing for her family since she was fifteen years old, always hustling to make a living so she could feed her children, never able to truly enjoy the joys of being at home with her kids. It seemed that the coming year, the jobs we'd lined up would finally allow her to stop and smell the roses—in this case the roses being her precious time with her children, another enormous spark of joy and hope for a better tomorrow that would never arrive.

The day of Jen's last concert, December 8, 2012, my family and I laid my father to rest in California. My dad had been on life support prior to passing, living at the hospital, with my siblings and me taking turns to be with him—I'm the eldest of six. And I was the strong one, because my dad expected me to be strong, so I took that role to heart in my family, just like Jen did in hers. Another reason we understood each other so well. In any case, that night, after the funeral, and after what would be Jen's last concert ever, she called to check up on me and see how everything had gone. She was really happy with the show and told me it had been fantastic. I was sorry I couldn't be there. She'd also hoped her dad and youngest son, Johnny, could've come, but due to work and school, they couldn't make it either, so we chitchatted for a while. She told me she was starving, which was the norm with her because she never ate before a concert and was always famished by the end of the night, so we said our good-byes and hung up. I never imagined that this would be the last conversation I would ever have with her in my lifetime.

As I got ready for bed, I remember telling my wife, "You know, tomorrow I just want to catch up on some football and have some comfort food." Even though I knew my father was going to die, losing someone you love still requires time to mourn and process it all. She and my family respected that and understood I needed that healing time. So we turned off the lights and went to sleep, but rather than sleeping in, I was jolted awake by our home phone ringing off the hook early Sunday morning.

While I processed the sound—our home phone hardly ever rung, everyone calls my cell phone, so hearing the landline was an anomaly—my wife gently nudged me and said, "The phone, the phone, you should go check the answering machine." As I rubbed the sleep out of my eyes, I automatically thought one of my aunts might not be feeling well—they were a bit older and they'd just buried their brother. I was almost afraid to go downstairs to check the machine. I knew it had to be something important, and I was afraid of hearing the message. When I pressed play, I was thrown. It wasn't any of my family members, but rather the voice of a good friend of mine in the business asking me to give him a call about Jen's plane. The following message was our agent at CAA calling to see if I could confirm the rumor that was circulating about her plane going down, and the next one was a good friend and Televisa executive calling me about the plane.

At first, I was in complete disbelief. I honestly didn't think it was true. In Mexico, if you're on a private plane, you're basically an hour away from anywhere in the country, and with Jen, we were used to getting on a plane after a show and flying to another city to attend an after party or meet friends for breakfast. Furthermore, in the United States you're required to register your destination when you take a private jet, but that wasn't the case in Mexico. There you simply hop on a jet as if you were taking a cab and tell the pilot where you want to go, and he'll fly you there. Knowing all this, as I heard the messages and all the commotion, instead of worrying, my first thought was honestly, *Damn Jen, she must have decided to go somewhere else.* The possibility of the plane actually going down wasn't even registering on my radar.

Still in shock, trying to process what was happening, another thought suddenly crossed my mind: *Maybe she'd been hijacked from the plane.* This wasn't unheard of in Mexico. Even Learjets land in the Sierra for the cartels, so the possibility of Jen being held hostage somewhere for ransom wasn't that outrageous. If that was the case, I knew Jen would expect me to move heaven and earth to find her and bring her back home, so I sprang into action. Jen trusted me, she knew that if she was ever in danger or trouble, I'd be the one to get her out of it, so I was ready to turn every rock over until I found her.

As the next hour ticked by, I continued plotting ways to get to Mexico and bring Jen back home. I was thinking of people I could call, digging up any and all connections I could come up with that could help me find her. However, my thoughts and plans were quickly interrupted by the incoming flood of calls from our staff. "What's going on?" "What should we do?" I honestly had no idea. I was fielding all these calls without knowing what to tell everyone because I wasn't sure myself what to think or believe.

Time flew by, 6:00 a.m. became 10:00 a.m. in a heartbeat, and we still didn't know where Jenni was. In another blink of an eye, I was sitting in her office at her house with all her staff, taking the lead, flying blind, trying to figure out what was going on. Everyone was looking to me to indicate what the next step should be, but I still didn't have a clue. Meanwhile, the family decided that they would all meet and wait for news together at Jen's mother's house, so when the kids left for their grandmother's place, we moved the staff headquarters from Jen's home office to my home. We settled in, not knowing that this would become our nerve center up until her memorial ten days later.

In the meantime, Televisa news reached out to me asking if there was any way we could hop onto a secure server line for them to share their newsfeed with us. That's when we saw the crash site. In that instant, everything suddenly switched gears. We went from a "we gotta find her" mode to a "we gotta bring her home" mode. I shared the news with the family, but they weren't willing to let go of their hope. It was all way too hard to come to terms with. So they stepped out of Mrs. Rivera's home and stood before the press, stating that they were still looking for her and that they would bring her back. They were still in denial, but back home we had already seen the feed. We had seen the shredded pieces of her clothes strewn around the site. She was gone.

Shaken by the news, I numbed my pain by diving into work mode and figuring out the next steps: identify her remains, bring her home, and plan the memorial. Meanwhile, a media circus ensued. The family kept making statements to the press outside their home, while the brothers were figuring out who would travel to Mexico to bring their sister home. Back at my place, behind the scenes, Julie had taken off back to Jen's house to grab one of her toothbrushes and some hair from her hairbrushes to give to the family so that they could identify Jen's body via a DNA sample. It was all so bleak. We then started fielding questions from Jen's siblings about her body. More than six hundred body parts had been found at the site, and they all needed to be tested to figure out if any of them belonged to Jen. Gustavo and Juan were the ones who flew down to Mexico to help bring this investigation to a close, but we knew more about Jen than they did. They kept calling us with questions.

"The coroner would like to know if my sister had back surgery," asked one of the brothers on the phone.

"No, she never had any back surgery," replied Julie.

"Well, the coroner is saying that this body part that they found is scarred and more than likely indicates that this person had surgery in their back."

As gruesome as this may all sound, we finally realized that what they were describing was the front part of her torso. She had had a hernia surgery that caused a scar in her abdomen. So we provided all this information in detail and helped confirm that that was indeed Jen's remains.

To top it all off, let's not forget that I had just laid my father to rest the day before. I still hadn't even had a chance to begin to mourn my dad when suddenly I was dealing with the shock of losing Jen. It was all too much, but as the eldest in my family, always looked upon for strength and protection, I somehow powered through. Not only did I have to be strong for my family, I suddenly also had to be strong for Jen until her accident was resolved and she was laid to rest in peace. I couldn't afford to break down, so as the news unfolded, I turned my emotions off and kept ploughing through this tragic outcome. Practical leadership skills went on high alert to get whatever was needed done and be as efficient as possible. It was almost like another major concert, another major event for her, but this time around she wasn't there to guide us. We had thirty-three employees who were heartbroken and lost, so I stepped in and manned the fort.

Now, as if taking the lead with my family, Jen's family, and our work family wasn't enough, we also couldn't forget about the other four families in Mexico who were also grieving a huge loss and had far less means to retrieve their loved ones' remains and give them the burial and peace they deserved. We also had her band devastated by the news and stuck in Monterrey, and they too needed to get home. There were so many moving pieces, so much going on at once, that in retrospect, I honestly have no idea how I managed to continue marching forward through some of the darkest days of our lives, but there was absolutely no room for weakness, so I focused on my main mission: we had to bring our girl back home.

Chapter 13

The Aftermath

Jenni Rivera ✔
@jennirivera

I love my J-Unit, fans, family and
true friends...because in the middle
of the madness..they "hold on".
#jenniFACT

11/2/12, 11:59 AM

539 RETWEETS **393** LIKES

After Jen's fatal accident, I was invited to a Rivera family meeting at Mrs. Rivera's house. Only Jen's parents and her siblings were present—no wives, no children. I was asked to join them to take Jen's seat and help them discuss what needed to be done. Jen's remains had been identified, so we were in the process of bringing her home and had to figure out what the next logical steps would be. I still felt dopey and numb inside, mourning my dad and unable to fully process Jen's death, so what I heard at this meeting left me somewhat flabbergasted. All I could think about was bringing Jen home and laying her to rest. All they could think about was business.

They were in the midst of planning a fifty-two-date tour, which they wanted me to pitch as the Rivera Dynasty Tour, and needed to figure out how much money it would bring in as well as the lineup of musicians. Lupillo would obviously be headlining the evening, but they still needed to find someone to close the show. Meanwhile, Jen's brother, Pastor Pete, chimed in with his own proposal. He said that if we managed to get every one of Jen's fans to donate just one dollar each, he could open a new church. I sat there and observed them in awe. I really couldn't believe what I was hearing. I honestly thought I would find a family in mourning, torn and heartbroken by this tragedy, lost and overwhelmed by the circumstances; instead, I found a family trying to figure out how to make their next buck.

As the meeting continued, Lupillo suddenly turned to me and said, "You know what? I'm jealous of you. I'm jealous of how much time you spent with my sister and how much you know about her, and how much you've shared with her." That was probably the most heartfelt, earnest, and genuine moment in that entire meeting. The pain seeped through Lupillo's eyes as he spoke. He'd been focusing so much on his career and establishing himself that he didn't have a chance to share as many quality moments with his sister, even less so given their sibling rivalry, so I got it. They'd finally reconciled, and now she was gone and he couldn't take back time or ask for a re-do. It was such a human sentiment, one of the few ones I experienced with the family. Maybe the rest of the family felt the same way, but at that meeting, all they managed to do was talk about themselves.

Meanwhile, Gabo had written to Rosie because he wanted to be with all of us, and in the e-mail, he said:

Rosie: I haven't been able to sleep lately, and I looked for your e-mail to write you and say:

I know the very painful and tumultuous times you must be experiencing!!

I know that all of you, like me, are people of FAITH, and that's what keeps us standing!!

And that all of you, like me, are waiting for a miracle.

And if that weren't to happen, to also thank God for the time He allowed us to be with her on Earth.

I know you were the person she loved the most on Earth, aside from her children, but you were the most special person to her, and that should make you feel great and proud of your wonderful sister.

Gabo also mentioned to Rosie that he wanted to be there for them during this difficult and painful moment. She replied thanking him for giving Jenni so much love and for giving them space. She said she'd let him know when she could see them. But that day never came. She never called.

Back at the family meeting, I finally gathered myself and spoke up, giving it to them as straight as I always did. First I looked at Pete. "Pastor Pete, where's your faith? Is your faith not in God or is it in Jen's fans? Why, at this time, would you challenge that? Shouldn't that be a challenge to God and your faith, who shall provide?" He sat back and said nothing. Then I directed myself to the entire family, "This isn't the time to be announcing a national tour. Yeah, I'll look into it. But ultimately, what are we doing about

Jen?" Where was their sense of mourning? Didn't they want to at least celebrate her life and legacy? I didn't understand how they could be so focused on looking for ways on how to profit from such a tragedy, so soon after it had happened. It really hurt and baffled me, but I was no longer dealing with Jen with the heart of gold. Now it was just her family, and they had other plans in mind for the future. Instead of thinking about what Jen might have wanted, all they could focus on was their own needs. The meeting was finally adjourned, but this would be the first of a long list of situations that would leave me rattled, distressed, and speechless.

Case in point: the arrival of Jen's remains. When the private jet carrying Jen's remains finally landed in Long Beach, California, during what should've been a somber moment, Gustavo—who'd gone to Mexico with Juan— couldn't stop posting comments on social media about all the helicopters and cameras surrounding their arrival. He was like a kid in a candy story with all that attention, smiling as they interviewed him. How can you smile? Your sister's body parts are in the plane behind you, and you're smiling? I couldn't stop shaking my head.

Then came the memorial service on December 19, 2012, another crushing day. I not only attended as one of the two nonfamily members who were asked to stand up and eulogize her, I had also been called up to orchestrate the event, and had been working on it with our team from my home headquarters after receiving confirmation that she had been in that fatal plane crash. Ever since her death, I had switched into automatic pilot, coordinating all the details of everything that would lead to Jen's last day on a stage and her final resting place.

After ten arduous and harrowing days, the time had come to memorialize Jen. That Wednesday, as my wife and I pulled up to the Gibson Amphitheater, I cast my eyes to the sky and noticed helicopters hovering above, anxiously awaiting Jen's last public appearance. We were running late, and I was stressed out, so I looked back down, opened the door, and climbed out of the car, trying to stay focused on the event ahead, when suddenly my wife turned to me and said quietly, "Look, she waited for you." I glanced in the direction she pointed with her head and saw the hearse. The back door was open and the funeral home employees were pulling Jen's casket out of the vehicle. It suddenly felt as if we were arriving together for one of her shows, walking into the venue as we'd done so many other times throughout the last ten years, except this time instead of exchanging a glance while she walked ahead of me, hearing her crack a joke or pray before her performance, instead of seeing her cascading hair and those big brown eyes filled with sadness and joy, what lay ahead of me was a casket rolling up the theater ramp with her remains. Then my wife grabbed my arm and whispered, "She waited for you, for this moment." Moved to the core, I continued walking behind Jen, and together we entered the backstage area one last time, Jen first and me following, as we had always done before. I was immersed in this extraordinary God-given moment when I was quickly jolted back to reality by a voice yelling out, "Nobody touches the casket!"

The family had hired outside security to guard her casket and make sure no one lay a hand on it, but I would be damned if I wasn't going to have one last moment with my sister by choice and bid her farewell in peace. I went up to the team, asked to have a few minutes, and thankfully, rather than arguing with me, they respectfully walked away and gave me a little privacy. Looking down at that coffin and knowing Jen was inside, rather than by my side laughing, arguing, chatting, was one of the toughest moments of my life. It was hard to come to terms with such finality.

After I said my one-on-one good-bye, I walked with heavy steps toward the Rivera family, my heart breaking over this loss, hoping to commiserate with them and find some form of comfort in the sorrow we all shared that day. However, to my utter dismay, when I reached the group, instead of finding solace, I found a bunch of women complaining about not having enough people to do their hair and makeup, as if they were prepping for a show. I was stunned. My wife noticed how disturbed I was by the entire scene, so she consoled me, knowing my distraught silence all too well. The rest of the day was somewhat of a blur, with bits and pieces haunting me to this day as grief-laden flashbacks.

I clearly remember Jen's brother, Juan, walking over to me, shaking my hand, and saying, "Thank you for all that you've done for my sister and for taking care of her." I could hardly muster a response. I also remember Martha Ledezma, her longtime product manager at Fonovisa, approaching me that day and saying, "Jenni fulfilled her promise. We were all together on my birthday. I just wish it wasn't under these circumstances." Jen had been planning a birthday party for Martha on December 19, but instead of celebrating Martha's day, we were mourning the loss of our dear friend Jen.

On the flipside, I also remember Jen's banda showing up from Mexico. Having played with her at every show for the past few years and having shared so many experiences on the road together, they came to mourn this tremendous loss as her work brothers. But instead of having the chance to sit back and lean on one another for support during this sad and painful time, the Rivera family suddenly asked them to hit the stage and play. I couldn't believe my ears. These guys had gone to mourn their music sister, they weren't emotionally ready to play; they were attending as guests, not performers, they didn't even have their banda outfits. And that's why the Riveras had invited them: to play and accompany the other artists. So now, suddenly, Julie was rushing around trying to round up some borrowed banda uniforms for them to put on and go out there and perform with Jen's casket. What was the family thinking?

They weren't thinking. They were just going through the moves as if this were any other one of Jen's productions. Maybe it was their way of coping, I don't know; I just can ascertain that it rubbed many of us the wrong way. As I reviewed the speech I had written for the ceremony, I was hit with another shocking request: there should be no crying while each speech is read on stage because this was supposed to be a celebration. What the hell? How could I not cry for what we had just lost only ten days earlier? I get the whole celebrating her life thing, but we should've also been able to openly mourn what we and the world had tragically lost at the memorial service. Needless to say, when I finally took the stage, I was so focused on trying not to cry I wasn't even able to get through my eulogy. Tears welled up in my eyes and I couldn't see or say the words. I mustered a few phrases through the overwhelming pain and emotion, and stepped down. It was all just too much. Her fans were sobbing, devastated; her kids couldn't keep it together on stage either. It was just an emotional mess, and I think trying to hold back such a natural emotion as sadness only made it worse for us all. Now was not the time to celebrate; we first needed to mourn. The celebration should've been left for later, one that would help perpetuate her legacy in the years to come, but that was eventually also sidetracked.

As I left the podium, tears streaming down my face, I just couldn't return to my seat in the audience. Breaking down publicly was just too hard for me to handle, so I headed backstage followed by my wife, my rock, always by my side supporting me through thick and thin. As I sat down and tried to pull myself together, I noticed Joan Sebastián, the renowned Mexican singer and one of Jen's musical inspirations, approaching us. He quietly sat down next to me, took his hat off, held my knee, and said, "I understand. I understand you." That simple phrase filled with love and comfort will forever be etched in my heart.

Suddenly, amid all the mayhem, I began to realize that Jen's beloved work family was now the forgotten family. There was a coldness in the way we were all treated that truly pierced my heart and really drove in the reason why she cherished her team as if we were family. Yes, we got paid for our work, but we always went above and beyond, because we loved her. She'd come over to my place for a home-cooked meal whenever she needed comfort. It was a place where she could let her guard down and just be, where she could cry and be taken care of without worrying about keeping it together for everyone else. We were all there for her, and she knew it. That's why the final hit we took would've been unfathomable to Jen.

Her burial was scheduled for New Year's Eve, but the Riveras had explained that they just wanted family present, so we weren't invited to attend. We would've loved to be there, but we understood and respected the reasoning behind this decision. Jen had given so much of her life to the public that it only made sense for this last moment to be a private one, especially for her adored children. We got it. It was definitely the right thing to do, but that's not how it went down. We later found out that aside from family, there were also banda and norteño groups playing, and they'd been allowed to bring their wives. So these complete strangers were able to spend those last moments with Jen while her team, her work family, the people who had seen her through endless ups and downs, had to sit this one out. When we heard of this, we were all so stupefied and aggrieved. It was a mind-boggling and relentless blow, and it went against every fiber of Jen's being.

Jen always treated her team as part of her family. We were at Rosie's wedding not because Rosie wanted us there, but because Jenni wanted us there. We attended baby showers for her family, and Jen would also be present at our life events, even hosting a baby shower for my wife and me. It went both ways with all of us. Even on Christmas, the epitome of a family holiday, Jen would always make time to stop by our homes, deliver gifts, and spend a little time with our families. That's why being shunned by her family after Jen's passing left us battered and speechless.

Now, let me be clear, no one here is denying that they are her family, her blood; no one can ever take that away from them. I'm not trying to compare myself to a biological brother, but her work family was also a key part of her life, and there's no denying that either, no matter how hard the Rivera family tried to silence us in the years to come. They fought tooth and nail to control her story and make sure that if anyone was to garner attention on her behalf, it would be solely and exclusively them. It was as if they were suddenly trying to bury us together with Jen, erasing us from their memories as if we'd never even existed. However, everyone who's anyone in this industry knows all too well that in order to succeed you need a damn good team backing you every step of the way. You just can't do it all on your lonesome.

When the family inherited Jenni's estate, everything was running smoothly, nothing was broken. Her team, which had been in place running things for a while, was loyal, we knew what we were doing, and we were all willing and able to continue working for our dearly departed friend. But once the memorial and burial were over, and the new year had begun, we quickly realized the family had other plans for us. No one would be left standing with them.

While Jen fretted over taking a break or retiring from the spotlight because of how that would affect her employees and leave them without their bread and butter, her family showed no concern. At the start of 2013, the Riveras decided to dismantle the team and assemble a new one. They let everyone go, everyone except me. I was the exception for what later became one calculated reason: I was still generating money for them. They couldn't afford to let me go just yet because they needed my help to understand each and every aspect of Jen's many business ventures and finances. So I was basically the last of the gatekeepers, the last man standing from a team of people who were part of building Jen's wealth and legacy. We knew what she wanted to accomplish and how she wanted to get it done, we knew how she thought and what she felt, but rather than keep us all on to help her live on through her music and various ventures, the family obliterated that possibility. Those years of meaningful and worthwhile experience meant nothing to them. They just wanted a clean slate, so they could move on and do whatever they saw fit, no questions asked. And that's exactly what they did. They went on to hire a new team, a "yes" team, one that never questioned anything they did, and, as the last of the old guard, I stuck out like a sore thumb. But I had the blueprints to Jen's career, so they still needed me around, for the time being.

Somewhat oblivious to the impending changes to come, I continued working with the family as I had always worked with Jen. I put them up to speed with everything that we had up and running, but also never hesitated to question their business decisions or their spending, and this rubbed them the wrong way. I knew how Jen thought. I knew if she needed coffee or tea just by looking at her schedule for the day. But they weren't used to this; they weren't Jen. All I wanted to do was help the Rivera family get organized and honor Jen's legacy, but after a while, I started realizing that there wasn't much else I could do other than comply with their requests.

At first they were all a bit lost. Rosie had been left in charge of Jen's estate, and she was honestly quite distressed. She had been promoted from little sister to CEO of a multimillion dollar business overnight. None of them had realized how much wealth Jen had accumulated over the years because she never bragged about it or flaunted it with excessive luxuries, so they were genuinely overwhelmed. I was in charge of passing on all my knowledge to both Rosie and Juan, her brother, but it was no easy feat. We're talking about two people who had no real business experience, so it was like training rookies for an impending professional game. To top it off, Juan, who had no personal career successes under his belt, suddenly went from battling drug and alcohol addictions to managing Jen's estate—eventually becoming vice president of Jenni Rivera Enterprises—and now the world was his oyster.

What I observed as 2013 unfolded worried me, so I reached out to Chiquis and asked if she'd have lunch with me. When Jen and Chiquis had their falling out the prior year, Jen decided to take Chiquis out of her will. So suddenly Chiquis was left not only dealing with the unresolved issues she had with Jen and the pain of losing her mother so tragically, but also with no say in her legacy or in the care of her siblings, children who had grown up seeing her as their second mom. Furthermroe, after Jen's passing, Chiquis and I weren't on talking terms. She held a grudge because I had decided against working with her and Angel and because I had sided with her mom during their whole debacle, but she still said yes to lunch. I was happy she'd accepted because I was truly concerned about her well-being. I knew she was a good girl, and I knew Jen would've wanted me to look out for her because Jen's love for her would always be stronger than any feud.

So that day in 2013, when we sat at the table, I cut straight to the chase, "Listen, Chiqs, just as I had told you before, my loyalty is to your mom, and that's why I couldn't work with you. And now I'm here to tell you that my loyalty still stands with your mom, and if this means going against your Uncle Juan and Tía Rosie for what's best for you guys as kids, I will do that, and I'll stand behind that because I know that's what your mom would have expected of me."

I opened up and wanted to make sure she knew she could count on me. Little did I know that she was taping our entire conversation without my knowledge. As soon as the lunch ended, I drove off and she took the unauthorized tape and showed it to Rosie and Juan. Obviously, they were pissed and later confronted me about the whole situation, but I stood by my words. "Absolutely right, I said that. You're absolutely right," I responded after their accusations. I had nothing to hide, and they took offense. I was just trying to protect Jen and what she would've wanted for her legacy and children, but it was becoming increasingly apparent that soon I would no longer be around to do right by her. Once the family had all the information they needed, they took the steering wheel and, by mid 2013, they let me go and began to drive the vehicle on their own, while I slowly crashed and burned inside.

I was suddenly hit with a twofold blow. Instead of taking the time to mourn my dad's and Jen's deaths, I had poured myself into helping the Rivera family keep the diva's ship from sinking, only to be brutally cut off once they had received what they needed. That was it, they were done with me. They wanted to take control of her story and bend it in their favor without having any of the old guard around to call them out on anything. And me? I just froze.

A year had gone by and I had yet to process the shock of everything that had gone down. My emotions were suddenly paralyzed, crippled by the weight of it all. I went cold in 2014, and something inside me completely shut down. What followed were two of the most intense years of my life, some of the most challenging times for my wife and children, a period I couldn't have survived without their love and support as well as that of my siblings and close friends. They all went the extra mile, trying to get through to me, pierce through the shield that I had built around my heart. My brother took me out to do the things I usually enjoyed. My wife planned a family vacation hoping that would help her break through to me and get me out of this deep funk. Her patience was extraordinary; I will never forget it and will forever be grateful to the way she stuck by me during such trying times. But nothing seemed to work.

Everyone kept telling me I had to simply let it all out and let it go, but I didn't know where to begin. I was terrified of losing control. I had no idea what to expect if I really let it all out. It was as if I were a volcano on the verge of erupting; I felt I could easily decimate the entire village of people that surrounded me. Until one day, it finally happened. I was sitting on a chair in my backyard playing with my dog, while my family was doing their thing inside the house, as I had done many times before. However, this time, something shifted within. I began to reflect on my situation and suddenly felt a crack in my frozen lake of emotions. At long last one lonesome tear took the plunge and slowly rolled down my dry cheek. It was like that first drop of rain dotting an arid landscape after a two-year drought, inviting a thunderstorm of emotions to pour out of me in a deluge of tears. I realized I didn't have to hold it in anymore. I didn't have to worry about someone seeing me break down. It was okay. My favorite dog was out there with me, sharing his unconditional love, my beloved family was inside, and in that precise instant, I finally felt safe. I could've filled my pool with the tears that came storming down my face that day. Out of all the scenarios I had played out in my mind, I never expected it to all come gushing out in my backyard on what felt like any other normal day. It was such an immense relief. The mourning had finally begun, one that I'm still dealing with to this day as I pour the story I have held within for so long onto these pages.

Meanwhile, no longer blinded by this colossal loss, as my pain subsided and I began to heal, thoughts about the actual accident began to cross my mind again. After Jen's death, I was often asked if I really believed it had been an accident. But at the time, I couldn't talk about it. I didn't want to tarnish her memory with conspiracy theories. Intentional or not, she was gone and there was no way we were going to get her back. However, after my emotional breakthrough, I felt this question deserved a better answer.

I had had access to privileged information about the plane crash and, truth be told, authorities were never able to definitively rule it an accident. Officials claimed that what brought the jet down was a Dutch Whirlwind, a condition where the plane loses control of its stabilizer and crashes into a mountainside; however, the evidence they found at the crash site was inconclusive. If the plane truly hit the mountainside at such speed, there should've been a crater indicating the exact place it crashed, but none was found. Also, if that were the case, then why were their belongings scattered across a three-mile radius, not only on the ground but also hanging from trees? It just didn't add up. After paying close attention to these details and taking a better look at how the debris was strewn across the landscape as well as their remains, I honestly think that the plane fell from the sky already in pieces, likely from an in-air explosion of some sort. And that to me did not seem accidental.

As I digested all this information, the first person that popped into my mind was Angel, Chiquis's boyfriend. After their tense confrontation, Jen used her social media platform to publicly shame and humiliate him. So we're talking about an influential man who felt strong animosity toward Jen and whose wife possibly had ties to powerful people in Mexico—that seemed like pretty good motive in my book. Suddenly, it all made sense, and I began to believe he might have had something to do with her untimely death. I mulled over this theory for quite some time, but finally laid it to rest in early 2016. Why? Well, because that's when I became privy to evidence that pointed to another unexpected direction: Mario Macías, Jen's attorney in Mexico, the man who had taken Gabo's place when he was let go, and one of the passengers on the plane who had also died in the crash.

Mario Macías was first recommended to us by our close associates in Mexico when Jen got stopped at the airport for carrying $50,000 that were allegedly undeclared. He helped sort out that mess and, after Jen and Gabo's fallout, Mario stepped in and began to take care of everything in Mexico for her. At the time, it made sense to us: he was a lawyer, he knew Mexico well, he understood the industry, so we thought he would be a good person to have on our side. And that's how he managed to wedge himself into a role on the team and Jen's inner circle. Then people started talking. Many said that in that time that Gabo was no longer on the team, Mario had started to change. Gabo himself heard about these rumors. He can't verify any of it, because they were after all rumors, but he did get word that Mario had started doing business with the wrong crowd.

As Gabo recalls: "With that type of job in Mexico, you find yourself interacting with a circle of very important people both within the music industry and the cartels, and you have to learn how to deal with them. I kept it simple. My business relationship with them was strictly focused on being the liaison between the artists I managed and the clients who wanted them to play at their venues or events. That was it. Rumor has it that Mario took these relationships to another level and made them more personal. And that's when those who were around him claim that he started to change. He was smug, treated many people poorly, and was rumored to be involved in personal business dealings with the cartels. Again, I can't confirm it, but it's what I've been told from several different sources."

When 2016 rolled around I really wanted to get to the bottom of all this. Still pretty convinced that Angel was a clear suspect, I finally hopped on a plane in July 2016 and traveled to Mexico to see what I could dig up. I hooked up with my old business associates and started poking around and discovered this new and unexpected theory on the ground. My connections assured me that, although Angel had the money, he didn't have the power to pull something like that off. He didn't have the necessary influence in Mexican territory to make such an "accident" happen. Funnily enough, that brought me peace. It was good to discover that Chiquis's boyfriend didn't go to such lengths for vengeance, but the question still remained: had it been an accident or not? And if not, who the hell was involved?

The new theory I gathered through my sources pointed to Mario Macías. He was also on that plane when it crashed and had also died on that tragic day. What I didn't know until this trip was that after the accident, authorities found Mario's car in Mexico City with close to $200,000 in cash stashed away in the trunk … and it was not Jenni's money. I also discovered, much to my surprise, that Mario had a military background, and it was rumored he had ties to Los Zetas, one of the most dangerous Mexican cartels whose members were all ex-military officers. Turns out we had no idea who Mario Macías really was. Not only did it seem he may have had ties with Los Zetas, but we also discovered that aside from his wife and child, he had another family hidden away, another woman and more children. This seemingly tough and conservative lawyer was leading a double life right before our eyes, and none of us had taken notice. Never had it crossed any of our minds that he could've been involved in personal dealings with the cartels. As if all this wasn't enough to point the finger in his direction, Monterrey is known as Los Zetas territory, and it was rumored that Mario's business with them had taken a turn for the worse and gone south quick. Maybe Mario had been the target all along, and Jen and the rest of the team were simply collateral damage.

Aside from also knowing that a couple of officers had been prosecuted for stealing evidence from the crash site, what further fed this emerging Mario Macías theory was some surveillance footage I was shown as Jen and the crew checked into the airport in Monterrey on that Saturday, December 9, 2012. In the video there are three SUVs arriving at the airport, Jen together with her production team and entourage. The lead vehicle stops at the guard shack, the security guard on duty walks up to the car, checks credentials, then heads over to the second vehicle to verify Jen's credentials, and then allows the three vehicles into the airport. As the last vehicle veers right and into the airplane hangar, another car pulls up to the guard shack. However, this one barely stops and instead passes right through, no credential check, no nothing. It was never logged in, and the guard, the only person who could've possibly identified the car and the people inside, resigned that night and vanished into thin air. No one was ever able to find him again.

Why did Mario have $200,000 cash stowed away in the trunk of his car in Mexico City? Why was that vehicle allowed to pass through airport security without being logged in? Where did the guard go? Why was there no crater in the mountainside where the plane had allegedly crashed? Why were the passengers' belongings scattered across a three-mile radius? No one was able to answer these questions, but it sure as hell doesn't look or sound like a plain old accident to me. Am I accusing anyone of murder? No. I'm just sharing what I discovered, a pile of inconclusive evidence that to me simply doesn't add up. Who knows if we'll ever know the truth behind Jen's fatal accident. All I know is that that crash took away my sister by choice, my friend, my ally, and it forever changed the existence of those of us who knew and loved and admired her. Meanwhile, Gabo decided to believe the news, that Jen and the rest of the passengers and crew had suffered a terrible accident and one of the wings was detached from the plane. He prefers to go with this theory; he doesn't want to believe that someone tried to hurt her by downing the plane. Gabo feels it was simply a tragic accident that took our sister away because that's the way God intended it to be. We will never be the same, but our memory of that kind, talented, witty, and generous human being will always live on within each and every one of us, our Gran Señora, our Diva, our butterfly, our friend.

We will never forget you,
Pete and Gabo

Epilogue

Jenni Rivera's Legacy

jennirivera
@jennirivera

"You are a WARRIOR. You have been one since before you were born...from within your mothers womb. It wasn't easy, but you survived. You always have. This WILL NOT be an exception. Get up and show the world that you don't fit in because you STAND OUT. Don't let what other people decide to do change who YOU are. WARRIORS keep on going....even after their injuries. You are not a 'fallen' soldier...get yo ass up and continue this war of life....God will take you to victory". #voicesinmyhead

2012-10-28

J en was the Helen Keller to Latina women. She didn't let any of her handicaps prevent her from succeeding in life. If I was to be asked to define her legacy, I would hope

257

that through her music, her life, and her imperfections, she's remembered as inspiring a generation to accept, embrace, and love themselves, and never quit on their dreams, aspirations, and goals. That was Jen. That was her struggle. No matter how many cards were stacked against her, no matter how many obstacles she encountered in her journey, she had the ability to rise up to each and every challenge and continue to push forward toward her dreams, and I know that's exactly what she would want every one of you to do too. Despite all the drama she had to endure, her message was one of hope. You can do anything you set your mind to, she was proof of that, and I know she would be ecstatic if her story served as an inspiration for you to accomplish your hopes and dreams.

And that's why I wrote this book. A lot has gone down since Jen's untimely passing. As the last four years unfolded, I noticed that her real story was marred by the need of those close to her, painting a picture of Jen that satisfied their necessities rather than celebrating her life, her struggles, her successes, and, ultimately, her legacy. When renowned singer Selena passed away, the world finally got to know her story at another level, and it inspired millions in establishing her legendary legacy, which still lives on to this day. That's what I want for Jen; however, when she passed, rather than bringing her story to the forefront, her family somehow closed her off from the world. They carefully controlled whatever information about her personal life was released, and rather than focus on her legacy, they chose to push their own personal stories onto her fans.

In the last four years, we've discovered who many of her family members are, but the fans haven't had much access to the wealth of inspiring experiences, struggles, and successes from Jen's own life. While everyone is using their angle of Jen's story to self-promote their own interests, her legacy has fallen by the wayside. I know for a fact that there's still plenty of music that could be released, from a duets album to a tribute album to tunes that have yet to see the light of day. Yet here we are, four years later, with only her Monterrey concert released as a three-part package, one volume per year with the last one out this year. Her fans deserve more.

Jen's fans were the fuel in her life. When things were looking down, she turned to them for love, comfort, and understanding. She poured her heart out on the stage, and they celebrated and supported her every step of the way. That's where Jen got her superpowers, in the presence of her fans; that's where she was truly unbreakable because they made her feel safe and loved. That's why she never took them for granted and never stopped thanking them, thanking them for their love, thanking them for helping her feed her family, thanking them for their loyalty. The stage and her fans were her safe haven, and that's why I feel her fans deserve more opportunities to help celebrate her life and continue to keep her amazing legacy alive and thriving.

I know her music will live on forever, and there will be many generations to come that will rediscover her songs and performances and fall in love with her on-stage presence, wit, and charm. So what I want to make sure is that we also never forget the person behind the music. The woman who celebrated her imperfections, the woman who, like many great leaders, put it all on the table to make her dreams a reality, while also never forgetting her humble beginnings.

Jen was born to lead. From her trendsetting style to her boundary-pushing career moves, she was a trailblazer in her own right. So what was her secret? What made her the successful and accomplished superstar who sold more than twenty million albums worldwide and garnered several gold and platinum records certified by the Recording Industry Association of America (RRIA)? Of course there was her relentless and tireless perseverance, but she couldn't have done it without her multigenerational legion of loyal fans. And how did she amass this army of supporters? It wasn't solely because of her music, it was also because of Jen's story, her struggles and her life as a single Latina mother. It was a story people could relate to. It was a story that reflected the lives of countless other women working tirelessly to make ends meet for their families. And it served as an inspiration to all of them, fueling their hope that anything and everything is possible if you put your mind to it, do the work, and never lose faith.

Many generations of Latinas can identify, even to this day, with some part of Jen's life. They understand what it feels like to face discrimination within a male-dominated society and industry, they know what it's like to have a body that's not considered a perfect ten by Western cultural beauty standards, they've been betrayed or even abused by the men they've loved, and many are fighting to survive as single mothers and put food on the table for their own children. They got it back when Jen first began to share her struggles and story, and they get it now as those same struggles are unfortunately just as real as before. Even in death, Jen's legacy continues to live in the hearts and souls of her fans who rose up and followed her lead after hearing the songs she wrote and performed, and that's why they still defend her so vehemently to this day.

From a media standpoint, many have yet to put their finger on Jen's magic. In her absence, Chiquis is being built up by the media, and people gravitate to her in hopes of finding pieces of what Jen had offered them, but it's not working because they're missing the point. What the media doesn't get is that Jen was truly multidimensional, so much so that many of her followers weren't even fans of her music! They were fans of her as a woman. Her older Puerto Rican, Dominican, and Cuban followers couldn't have cared less about banda music, but they absolutely adored Jenni Rivera. Why? Because they'd seen her tell her story on Don Francisco or Cristina Saralegui's shows, and they were hooked. Finally, there was a Latina celebrity doing the media rounds who wasn't a perfect ten and owned it, who was a single mother and wasn't afraid to share the struggles that this role entailed, who'd been betrayed and abused and was transparent enough to share her story. She became a voice for a multitude of multigenerational women with different causes, their reigning queen, and that was the key to her success.

No one can replace Jen's story, her substance, her honesty, her charm. She wasn't afraid of challenges, she broke down many barriers, and she learned from her mistakes. So much so that prior to her life coming to its tragic end, she was even learning how to choose better suitors, men who were actually worthy of her love and kindness and passion. One specific gentleman who was courting her was a good-looking, refined, top-level executive at a major beverage company in Mexico. She'd nicknamed him Mr. Coca-Cola. He'd call her and leave voicemails of him serenading her while playing the piano. Jen would listen to these serenades in disbelief. Having such a successful entrepreneur courting her, a single mother, now even a grandmother, in such a classy way was all so new to her, she sometimes wondered out loud, "Am I deserving of this?" It was difficult for her to accept and believe that yes, she could attract such a great guy, and yes, she most certainly deserved it. Of course she was scared, how could she not be? As she used to say herself, her heart was like a broken mirror, scarred by all the cracks, but she could still see her reflection, and she was still standing. And after having endured so much pain, it was great for her self-esteem to attract such deserving attention. After taking such a beating to her heart, it was the start of something that would've helped her heal. It reminded her of her worth when all bets were against her.

Although most people saw her as the glorious butterfly she had visualized for herself, Jen actually still felt she was in the metamorphosis stage, not quite the butterfly she wanted to be yet, but inching closer every day. If someone was to ask me if she had any regrets before leaving this earth, I'd say it was that she didn't fully enjoy her success. She was a workhorse who was never able to fully embrace and enjoy everything she'd accomplished. Her ghosts of the past continued haunting and chasing her and never allowed her to stop and truly smell the roses of her life's work. Nevertheless, at the time of her passing, there had been a shift in Jen, one that was allowing her to acknowledge that she had earned the great experiences making headway in her life. She was learning to forgive herself and finally embrace the happiness she could see rising like the sun at dawn over the horizon, inching closer to the serenity she'd dreamed of for so long, one that she finally reached with her passing.

Jen is at peace now, so the time has come for us to close this chapter and move on. I only hope that you not only remember all of Jenni Rivera's success, but also all the times she fell, because that was when she became our true beacon of light. Her strength and resilience are the example we should all live by. We're all going to make mistakes, we're all going to fall, but what matters is how we rise after every stumble in our journey.

If Jen has taught us anything, it's that no obstacle, no matter how big or small, should stop us from going after our dreams, and no amount of fame should prevent us from helping others along the way. In the end, Jenni Rivera's story was a universal one of love, loss, and the struggle to survive. It's up to you to live the life you desire and deserve. Let Jen's journey be your guide. Her life may have ended abruptly and senselessly, but her music and her legacy will live on forever.

Acknowledgments

T
o my longtime friend, Anthony R. Lopez, who was responsible for introducing me to Jenni, someone she referred to as "Attorney of my Life." You have been more than a friend and inspiration to all those who have worked with you.

To all those who worked as a team for Jenni from its early years and until the end: Gabriel Vásquez, you and I witnessed a lot along this journey. No one will ever know what you endured to assure Jenni got the best. Giselle "Gigi" Jara, our first fulltime makeup artist, from our first encounter with you at LATV we knew you were special. Hector "The Protector," you were more like a son to her, and you were the anchor to the road crew, bringing everyone comfort and security. Yanalté Galván, as Jenni's first publicist you showed so much passion and determination. Laura Lucio, you were not only Jenni's media consultant, you were her friend. Veronica Nava, girl, you were the best friend and homegirl.

To Ivan Montero, her original stylist; Adan Terriquez, her longtime designer and friend; M&M Group, the Scafutos, for believing in us and booking her in casinos when no else would. To her family at Universal Music, Gustavo Lopez, Martha Ledezma, José Behar, Victor Gonzalez, Miguel Torres.

To Julie Vásquez, you were more than her personal assistant, you were her glue.

To Fern Dogg, I think we all know that you were soul mates. I am glad to be your homeboy and friend.

To Grupo Desatado, you were there early on and shared so many memories from the road. Washa and Banda Divina, you guys were the team.

To the team members who took the journey with her to heaven: Arturo Rivera, Jacob Yebale, Mario Macías, Jorge "GiGi" Sanchez, you all made the ultimate sacrifice, and you shall never be forgotten.

And to my family, Jesse, Val, Maria, Eddie and Christina; my partner, Gloria, *mi amor,* you were the anchor in a difficult time; my kids, Elias, Mark, Ivan, and Jocelyn; and to every single fan who has supported Jenni throughout the years. I am forever grateful.

—Pete Salgado

First and foremost, I would like to thank God for putting us on the same path and joining us in this great adventure called Jenni Rivera. It was a journey we traversed together, hand in hand, with ups and downs, stumbling and getting back up again, with adversities and abundance, and above all many blessings. Thank you, Jenni, for allowing me to be your friend, your manager, your confidante, your brother—as you so often called me. You have no idea how much we miss you here on Earth, but we know that you're doing much better than us up there in God's presence. I know that's why you left us here, to give us the chance to tell your people and fans the woman, singer, mother, sister, daughter, and friend that you were. You know you don't just belong to a few people, you belong to your people, your audience, and to all of us who love and will continue to love you.

I also want to thank Pete Salgado, Julie Vásquez, César Ramirez "Chicharo," Ariel Rivas—we started out together—Jacob Yebale, Arturo Rivera, Mario Larios, Cinthia Rivera, Grupo Desatados, Tu Banda Divina, Chavita, Yanalté Galván, Laura Lucio, Danny Ramos, and all the people and media who supported us and were part of this extraordinary journey called Jenni Rivera.

I will always remember you and forever carry you in my heart.

With all my love and respect,

–Gabriel Vázquez Aguayo

About the Authors

Pete Salgado, a Los Angeles native and businessman, was Latin icon Jenni Rivera's manager, as well as creator and executive producer of *I Love Jenni, Welcome to Los Vargas*, and *Jenni Rivera Presents: Chiquis 'n Control*. Salgado is an established entertainment industry executive who has developed careers for recording artists, actors, and publishing companies.

Salgado met Jenni Rivera in 2003, and in the following ten years, he not only served as her manager, he also became her "fifth brother," as she would so often say when referring to him. As her trusted friend, Pete stood by Jenni and counseled and guided her through several divorces, family trials, media scandals, legal strife, as well as life and death scenarios. When Jenni suffered deep blows to her self-esteem, Salgado served as her backup, while also witnessing her amazing strength of character, resilience, and determination to prevail by any means necessary.

In the aftermath of Jenni's untimely passing, Salgado comes forward to openly share the details of Jenni Rivera as he knew her. *Her Name Was Dolores* is his way of honoring Jenni's final request: "If anything happens to me, you know what to do." In Salgado's words, "The publishing of this book not only celebrates the life of a woman who stood for all women as a warrior of the truest kind, but also creates a space for me to, years later, finally begin to heal. NO ONE made Jenni or her career; she was destined to be our star and we were all fortunate to be part of it."

Salgado currently manages former World Champion Boxer Fernando Vargas and award-winning Latin pop artist Frankie J, owns several lifestyle and entertainment companies, and is the CEO and founder of Tuyo Media Group. He lives in Los Angeles, California.

G abriel Vázquez Aguayo is a producer, musician, and writer, with twenty-five years of experience in the entertainment industry. He is also a creative director specializing in management and marketing, as well as a worldwide renowned concert producer. Gabriel worked with Jenni Rivera from 2000 to 2011 and was a key member of her team, responsible for breaking her into the Mexican market. He currently lives in Mexico.